Secret Di
Past & Present

ԑᴑᴄ𝔅

Q&A

with

Helena Whitbread
&
Natasha Holme

Table of Contents

Introduction

In January 2013 two women met in the upstairs room of a small café in Brighton, to discuss a subject dear to both their hearts: diary-keeping. Given their forty years' age difference, their backgrounds, and their lifestyles, Helena Whitbread and Natasha Holme had very little else in common.

Their approach to the form differed in that Helena is a reader and editor of diaries while Natasha is a diarist herself. The focus of their meeting was on two specific diaries which, although separated by almost two hundred years, nevertheless had a common bond: both were written in an esoteric code in order to conceal the same secret — that of their lesbian sexuality.

Of the two diaries under discussion, the historical one was written by Anne Lister (1791-1840) who has become known as the first modern lesbian, and the second is the work of Natasha Holme herself.

Helena Whitbread

I was born in 1931 into an Irish-Catholic family and have lived all my life in or near my home town of Halifax, a Pennine town in West Yorkshire.

Due to ill-health I left school at the age of thirteen and was sent to the east coast for a six-month stay with relatives. I never returned to school. Back home in Halifax at the age of fourteen, I began my working life of unskilled jobs in offices, shops, and factories.

Aged eighteen, I began to train as a children's nurse, but again ill-health prevented me from fulfilling the course. I married at twenty-one and had a family of one son and three daughters.

Although happy in my family life, my interrupted education plus my abortive attempt at the nursing profession had instilled in me such a sense of failure that I had resigned myself to limited options so far as my working life was concerned. I did, however, become an avid reader.

While working as a barmaid in my local pub, I overheard a university student who was drinking with a group of his friends. He told them that he was reading *The Doll's House* by Chekhov. I, reprehensibly, murmured, 'Don't you mean Ibsen?' The young man was understandably annoyed and questioned how a barmaid would know about such things.

The following evening, the student returned to the pub and said, 'I owe you a pint and an apology. You were right. But if you are reading Chekhov and Ibsen what are you doing working as a barmaid?' I replied that I wasn't clever and had left school at thirteen. He assured me, 'If you are reading Norwegian and Russian playwrights, you are clever. Get up to the Technical College and get on with your education.'

I took his advice and after three years of study I had obtained sufficient qualifications to gain entry into the Civil Service as a tax officer in the Inland Revenue. After eight years in that post I became restive and enrolled in the Open University for one year, leading to full-time study at Bradford University, where I obtained a degree in

Politics, Literature and the History of Ideas, gaining a 2.1 B.Sc (Hons). A further year's study took me into the teaching profession.

However, I wanted to be a freelance writer, and it was this ambition which brought me into the world of secret diaries. I had decided that my first research project would be about the life of a local woman, Anne Lister, who had lived in Halifax almost two hundred years earlier. I had no idea what I would discover.

Anne Lister (1791-1840)

Anne Lister was a wealthy nineteenth century landowner and diarist, who believed that she had developed an uncrackable secret code. One sixth of her diaries was written in this code, to which she referred as her 'crypthand.' However, Anne's code was cracked by a family member in the 1890s, and what those passages contained was scandalous: details of her emotional and sexual involvement with other women. The discovery of Anne Lister's lesbianism was kept secret, and was certainly unknown to Helena Whitbread when she began the study of Anne's journals in the 1980s.

Born in Halifax, West Yorkshire on the 3rd April 1791, Anne Lister was the second of six children, four sons and two daughters. Three of the sons died at early ages. The fourth son died from drowning whilst serving in the army. It was by virtue of the untimely deaths of her brothers that Anne, as an adult, was able to become the eventual heir to the Halifax family home of Shibden Hall and its estates.

From the age of fifteen until six weeks before her death on the 22nd September 1840 at the foot of the Caucasian mountains in

Russia, Anne kept a voluminous journal which ran to 6,600 pages and almost four million words. She detailed every aspect of her colourful and adventurous life.

It is through the medium of her journals that we are allowed to witness her development not only as a landowner, businesswoman, intrepid traveller and lover of women, but also the strategies she employed in the construction of her sexual identity.

Her journals became an emotional outlet and a psychological prop for Anne and, inadvertently, provided the foundation for a literary masterpiece which has now found its place in the canon of other famous English diaries. In 2011 the journals of Anne Lister were recognised by the United Nations as a pivotal document in British history and were added to the United Kingdom Memory of the World Register for documentary heritage of UK significance.

Natasha Holme

I was born in 1969 into a right-wing, middle-class family. My father was a Christian who believed every word of the Bible, my mother an ex-Christian who was almost constantly either ragingly angry, or on the verge of anger.

My younger sister and I teamed up to protect ourselves against our parents, attempting to run away from home together twice when we were very young. We used to beg our father to divorce our mother and take us away from her. Our father, however, was terrified of his wife, and claimed that as a Christian he had to remain married to her.

I yearned for the love of a gentle mother and so turned my affections to female teachers at school.

Christianity was a subject of fear in my life. I became obsessed with researching alternative religions and philosophies in order to escape it. Under the influence of Bible study and the Christian holidays that our parents sent us on, I did not relax easily into my burgeoning lesbian sexuality.

My obsession with diary-writing had a slow start in my early teens. However, fortuitously, I was enthralled by foreign languages, six of which I studied at O Level (French, German, Spanish, Italian, Latin, and ancient Greek). Having learned Greek I had the base for a secret code in which I could record the desperate love I felt for my French teacher, Miss Williams, throughout my school years and beyond.

Needing to record my feelings, and having developed a code with which to hide them, diary-writing became a daily, detailed, time-consuming habit, to which I am still addicted in my forties.

Having written towards nine million words (by summer 2016), vastly more than both Anne Lister (four million) and Samuel Pepys (one million), I must be among the most prolific diarists in the history of the world.

I have published three books from my diaries, between the years 1983 and 1991, covering my unrequited love for my school teacher, my bulimia, and misadventures on my year abroad in Boulogne-sur-Mer, France.

'Natasha Holme' is a pseudonym.

Helena

When I first heard that you have been keeping a diary from a young age and, furthermore, that you had used an esoteric code, I was immediately interested. I was further intrigued by the fact that you are a lesbian and wrote about your sexual life. It seemed to me that a modern parallel could be drawn with Anne Lister, the early 19th century lesbian diarist who had written a great deal about her lesbian sexuality in her journals, couched in a secret code of her own devising. I thought it would be interesting to see how far this hypothesis could be taken and wondered if you would be willing to join me in an exploration of the similarities and differences, as diarists and as lesbians, between yourself and a woman who lived some two hundred years before your time.

Natasha

I was thrilled to learn in 1990, aged twenty, about your work on Anne Lister's diaries. It was at a time when I was struggling cluelessly with my sexuality and was obsessively recording my feelings and behaviour around that. It seems to me that I wrote with the same sense of urgency as Anne, and in at least as much detail. I too chose to conceal myself behind a code. It is striking that, of the two of us, she who lived two hundred years ago was the one who was at peace with her sexuality, with a strong sense of personal identity, and who could almost be said to be an 'out' lesbian. I would love to explore with you the similarities and differences around Anne's and my approach to our sexualities, our respective motivations for the obsessive recording, and the ways in which we managed such a feat.

∽ ✿ ∾
Early sexuality

Helena

In your journals I see that you fell in love with Miss Williams, your school teacher, at the age of twelve, a passion that lasted throughout your school years and beyond. Anne Lister fell in love with fellow pupil Eliza Raine when she was fourteen and, as they shared a bedroom at their boarding school, Anne was able to quickly convert her love for Eliza into a sexual relationship. You, for obvious reasons, could not do this with Miss Williams. The questions I want to ask around this issue are:

- **Did you recognise your feelings for Miss Williams as sexual, or was it a case of 'heroine worship'?**
- **If the former, did you have sexual fantasies about her?**
- **Did you ever have such feelings about a fellow-pupil — girl or boy — of your own age?**

Natasha

I attended an all-girls, fee-paying, senior school for seven years. In my first year, when I was twelve, our French teacher was leaving to have a baby. At the end of the spring term of 1982 she brought her replacement into the class to meet us. This was Miss Williams, who would become our new French teacher following the Easter holidays. At the age of twelve I fell in love with this woman at first sight. I remember having the thought that if she did not reappear after the Easter holidays, then I would have to spend the rest of my life looking for her.

I recognised my feelings as romantic — very much so. I was completely in love with her, and I knew it. However, it was beyond me to feel sexual at that age nor, indeed, for many years afterwards. I had left school before I allowed myself to fantasise about even kissing Miss Williams. And I was shocked at how intensely aroused I felt when I did this.

I had taken on a lot of homophobia, particularly Christian homophobia, and I felt at that time that if I touched another woman, I would ruin her life — a view which was, obviously, crippling to my sexual development. This dysfunction led to some obsessive and wacky behaviour.

What I felt for Miss Williams was not 'heroine worship.' She was sweet, kind, gentle, vulnerable — not a 'heroine' figure.

I also had a huge crush on one of the girls who was my best friend when I was twelve and thirteen. My possessive behaviour towards her led her to break our friendship at the end of the second year. I was in a lot of pain over this. For two years I cried myself to sleep. Again the feelings were 'romantic.'

Anne had an erotic life at a young age. My experience was one of protracted, wistful yearning. My feelings went unexpressed — sexually, at least. Similarly, into our twenties, Anne had passionate love affairs, whereas mine were stifled. I didn't start relaxing into my sexuality until I was in my thirties. I am endlessly amazed and full of admiration that a lesbian living two centuries before me could be more 'out and proud,' more positive and carefree about her sexuality than I, who was born into an era of relative sexual freedom.

--- Anne's early sexuality ---

5.12.1809

[Love letter to Eliza Raine, copied into her diary]

How my heart throbs for thee ... Here I turn my eyes to my bed.
This, I hope, after a few years, which confidence in your affection
will shorten, you will share with me & thus complete my worldly
wishes. Never did I feel, as on Friday night, you were continually
before my eyes. I could scarcely believe you were not with me & yet
when I stretched out my arms you were not there. In the warmth of
my affection I almost cursed our separation & declared to myself
that I would rather die than live long without you.

29.10.1824

[I] Said I had had no theory till of late years. It was all practice. I had
become attached at fourteen. Described poor Eliza Raine. Alluded to
my acquaintance with Miss Alexander; my being very giddy; Eliza
getting to know it & the break-up of all but friendship.

13.8.1825

... talked to my Aunt about Eliza Raine. Somehow or other speaking
of her many qualities. Said, when my Aunt spoke of the danger poor
Sam might have been in, the danger was not to him but, like the
stag, they all turned their blind side to the water whence the danger
came & [I] said it was not my fault Eliza & I did not go off together.
Bade her never name it ... In excuse, said I was fifteen at the time.

29.5.1828

Telling [Miss MacLean] of my inclination to have gone off with Eliza Raine to the banks of the Arno but waited for her to come of age & was harum-skarum. She doubted me, fretted, etc., & the thing went off. She became insane.

--- Natasha's early sexuality ---

Friday 19th October 1984, Home

Miss Tennyson said, "I don't expect you to write 'fuck off' on desks, or 'fucking, sodding bitch,' or suggest that any member of staff is sexually ... strange."

We couldn't believe it and we were trying not to burst.

She said, "'Fuck' isn't a word you should use for something that is supposed to be a *beautiful experience.*" That was lovely. I nearly fainted. I haven't heard anyone speak so plainly. Especially Miss Tennyson.

Then:

"Do you know what the word 'sodding' means? Hands up if it's just a swear word to you?" (Everyone puts their hands up) "Does anyone know what it means?" (No hands) "Then I presume you use it out of ignorance. It is the most *repulsive* word and I cannot believe you'd use it if you did know the meaning. I suggest you look it up in the dictionary."

I did. It took me ages to find out. It was under 'sodomy.' She wasn't joking. It's disgusting.

Saturday 23rd August 1986, Home

Came back from Girl Crusaders Camp yesterday. I am so sad. If I have another Camp, I shall have a nervous breakdown. I love Ruth. She's fantastic. I dreamt about her, so she must be. I'm so sad, but that's OK because I'm only happy when I'm sad.

I spent last night crying because I miss Camp so much. I couldn't stop. It's only through love that I'm so sad. Surely that's wrong?

How did I know that Ruth played the cello? Weird. Because if I love someone, I know their mind.

I don't really know what else to write about Camp. I just want to explain more about Ruth. She is nineteen, a vicar's daughter, and she's lovely. I never really said goodbye to her because I had no idea what she thought about me.

[...]

Oh, why didn't I just say something to Ruth, tell her that I'd miss her or something? Anything. I totally botched it up. Maybe one day I'll meet her again and everything will be OK.

Wednesday 5th August 1987, Girl Crusaders Camp, Tirabad

Miss Cooke led the Bible study. Very interesting. About sex and gays.

In the afternoon we went on a car ride.

This evening I asked Miss Cooke if I could talk to her about the Bible study. She said tomorrow!

Thursday 6th August 1987, Girl Crusaders Camp, Tirabad

Had talk with Miss Cooke!! We went to a little town, sat in a café and had a drink. I told her. Honestly! And I cried. She said it used to be called "Pash," meaning "Grand Passion." Sweet, huh? She is now praying for Miss Williams.

14

❧ Physical diaries

<u>Helena</u>

Let's discuss the materiality of keeping such lengthy diaries. I think that the significance, to the diarist, of keeping a journal or diary can be gauged by the choice of paper or notebooks for the purpose of recording their daily life. The physical appearance of Anne Lister's journal indicates the growing importance of the role it came to play in her life. Her earliest entries, crammed into ten loose sheets of paper, cover the period from Wednesday 11th August 1806 to Thursday 22nd February 1810.

There is then a gap of three years until the appearance of a fragment of what was obviously a later attempt, a loose page dated merely March 1813. These eleven pages form a very rudimentary unbound journal. In 1816, following a further three year gap, Anne appears at some point to have taken up her journal more seriously. The former haphazard loose sheets are replaced by a succession of sturdy, hard-backed books, twenty-four in all. There is a similarity to these books which indicates that she bought them all from the same supplier, Whitley, the local bookseller and stationer in Halifax. Between the covers of these books, Anne's life is chronicled in minute detail.

Natasha

There are some striking similarities here, both with my own diary-keeping progression and with the physical aspects of the books in which I wrote.

My first efforts at keeping a diary began rather humbly inside an A4 ruled *Muppet Show* pad that I received one Christmas as a child. They are written in pencil, with no attempt at continuity or encoding. The very first entry is simply dated '1978,' when I would have been eight years old, and outlines a family holiday in Oxford.

No further entry occurs in this pad for three years. Then from Saturday 21st February 1981, when I was eleven, the entries are sporadic, with several weeks or months between them. I recorded what was number one in the Charts, that I was busy with a school project, and that I was planning to save my artwork.

By the age of fourteen I was recording my first cigarette, an unsatisfactory dating experience with a pupil at the boys' school, and noting down a number of lesbian crushes, mainly on teachers at school.

I was now using a padlock for privacy, having drilled holes through the *Muppet Show* pad. I often recorded how much I enjoyed reading back over the diary. My entries became increasingly obsessive, both in volume and in attraction to females. The last entry in the *Muppet Show* pad is Saturday 23rd August 1986.

At this point, my world of lesbian infatuation centred firmly around school. From Thursday 9th October 1986 I was using my school homework diaries as my personal diaries. The first entry that I disguised in code was the recording of a homophobic remark made by a teacher, who alluded to the word 'gay' and quickly added "not in an unpleasant way." This remark sparked an obsession with encoded diary-writing which, in summer 2016, is approaching nine million words — over twice the number that Anne Lister wrote.

From that entry onwards, I used a code based on the Greek alphabet. I was one of only three girls in my year who took ancient Greek for O Level, so using that alphabet as a base for the code felt safe. My entries were by now daily and ran into hundreds of words.

The school homework diaries were A5 in size and had red covers. I used four of these in all. At university I moved onto sturdy, hard-backed books — twenty-five in all. I bought almost all of the sturdy, hard-backed diaries from the same local stationers in my home town, as did Anne. They were made by a variety of companies, but were always 9" x 7", all ruled, and usually with a black, red, or blue cover. The number of pages ranged from 160pp to 320pp.

I was by now often writing thousands of words per day. Unlike Anne (who wrote only her lesbian intrigues in code), I now wrote everything in code but, like Anne, I wrote daily and in minute detail.

My diary-keeping has not been continuous. I became so obsessed with writing more and more that I ran out of time in which I was able to record it. I attempted to resolve this by declining invitations, doing less, trying to freeze my mind from thinking, so that I would have less to write up. It didn't work.

By May 1993 I was a few days behind. I started taking amphetamines to keep myself awake, to try to catch up. Again I hit failure — partly because of the volume of backed-up experience to record, and partly because the drug experiences themselves needed recording.

After four days and nights without sleep, I was hallucinating. There was a giant spider in the corner of the bingo hall where I worked, and my home town was on fire out of the window. The effects of the drugs made me write in more and more detail, too. My head cracked when I realised I couldn't keep it up. It was a horrific realisation for me at the time.

I wrote my diaries by hand until the end of 1995 (around three million words). Then I switched to computer in 1996 (approaching six million words as of summer 2016). Using a computer is so much faster and more efficient. I have been writing daily in minute detail again for many years.

--- Anne's hard-backed diaries ---

--- Natasha's hard-backed diaries ---

ᏪᏪ
Keeping a diary whilst
away from home

<u>Helena</u>

Anne wrote her journal up daily when she was at home but when away from home there could be problems. When on the road, travelling by coach, she would keep a little notebook, or sometimes a slate, on which she could jot down her impressions, e.g.

> *'Extracting some memoranda from a little red morocco pocket case with asses' skin leaves that was Eliza Raine's, previous to rubbing out all the writing & using the case in common for memoranda notes made on the spot for my journal. This plan will save me much trouble & I shall always be sure as I travel along that my observations, when made at the instant, are correct, at least as far as they can be so.'* [Journal entry 2.9.1822]

Can you describe the methodology you employed in keeping up the entries of your diary, particularly during travelling or when away from home?

<u>Natasha</u>

I always carried my diary with me — even when back-packing abroad. I wrote it in any spare moment (as well as rudely, when in company). I would conceal myself in toilets and stay up half the night.

I have only had to take notes when I've needed to be secret, for example on a date. If unable to take notes and I hear something which I want to recall precisely, I repeat it continuously in my head.

These days, when in company, I keep on top of my diary-writing on my mobile phone. No-one knows this. Observers would assume that I was texting or checking something out online. Technology has made the life of an obsessive diarist so much easier.

--- Anne's diary whilst away from home ---

30.8.1822

[On leaving home for a visit to Paris]

... The pewter bottle I had cast for my writing desk, I was obliged to leave. Just in time at 9 last night, [I] discovered the ink oozing out of a small flaw in the casting. I am determined to make neither difficulties nor disappointments. I shall put ink in one of the glass bottles in my dressing box.' [Once on board the steam packet taking her to France] 'I am writing at my ease, tho' there is a trembling sort of motion quite new to me at my writing desk.

19.6.1819

All the morning from 8 to 4½ (except from 9½ to 10¾ at breakfast & downstairs) arranging & copying out on loose paper my journal of Wed. 12 May – from London to Boughton hill – the pencil so bad to make out, & the order so confused – not to be wondered at, considering it was written on the box with the coachman. In the afternoon a little before 5, went to sit downstairs, & copied into my journal book about ½ what I had written on loose paper.

--- Natasha's diary whilst away from home ---

Sunday 25th November 1990, Paris

I shared a bus stop with a tramp to write my diary.

৪০৫
Keeping a diary in the age of technology

<u>Helena</u>

Anne Lister lived in an era in which there was no knowledge of today's technology. Pen, ink, and perhaps pencil and chalk for her rough notes were the only writing tools at her disposal. I don't think that today we would use a phrase such as …

> *'They little ween this ink shed of my pen.'* [Journal entry 22.7.1823]

At night and during winter afternoons, in the absence of adequate lighting, Anne wrote by candlelight and had only one precious copy of her writings.

How do you think your modern-day *modus operandi* contrasts with hers in the writing of your journals?

<u>Natasha</u>

I imagine Anne must have felt haunted by the fear of losing her recorded life. In the early years, photocopiers allowed me to keep a copy of every single page of my diaries. I had carrier bags full of them, which I kept in different towns (home and university) in case of theft or damage.

Recording my diary by computer, I can write in even more minute detail because touch-typing is so much faster than hand-writing. I have more accessible information at my disposal. I include my text messages. I can copy and paste whole (emailed) letters. What I can now do in seconds took me huge chunks of a day before.

I back up my diary files to an external hard drive and to Dropbox. I also email them to accounts on servers in different countries. Some years ago I spent several days scanning in and chronologically ordering the old carrier bags full of photocopies of my handwritten encoded diaries and backing them up digitally, too. All my diaries are now safe until the planet dies. I like to think that there is some kind of spiritual record-keeping entity, along the lines of the Akashic records, that will preserve them even then.

I encountered this concept of the Akashic records in my current work as a complementary therapist. These records are believed to contain every thought and deed that has ever occurred. They are held on the astral (non-physical) plane, through which the soul passes on its way to physical birth and after death. The records are encoded in astral light, and can be interpreted by clairvoyants.

So, in the absence of photocopiers and the internet, did Anne go to any lengths to keep her diaries safe from loss? Did she fear losing them?

Helena

So far as I can ascertain, Anne kept her completed journals locked away in her small study next to her

bedroom at Shibden Hall. When paying visits to her friends or on more extended travels she would take the current journal with her so that she could write it up daily. On those occasions she was usually very vigilant about the security of her journal, but in one instance she feared that it had got lost in transit.

In early April 1820 Anne and her married lover, Mariana Lawton, were staying with their friends, the Priestleys, at Haugh End in the village of Sowerby, about four miles south-west of Halifax. On their departure, Anne sent ...

'the manservant going before us with my bandbox (containing, besides clothes, letters [Mariana] had had from me since 1817, which she gave me this morning & my journal book).' [Journal entry 14.4.1820]

The manservant left the box at the Sowerby turnpike where it would be collected by the mail coach and dropped off at the White Lion inn at Halifax. As soon as Anne got to Halifax, she sent her manservant, Thomas, to the White Lion for her box.

'No tidings of it. Sent off a man to Sowerby turnpike to know if it had been sent by the mail. In great perturbation about it, but said nothing to my uncle.' [ibid]

The next day ...

'Told my troubles about the loss of my box ... Set off to Halifax — called at Northgate [the home of her Aunt Lister, widow of her deceased uncle, Joseph Lister] — still no tidings of my box. Went to the White Lion & desired Jenkinson [the innkeeper] to mention it in the waybill. Back again to Northgate. Wrote a few lines to the proprietor of the mail coach that runs from Halifax to York, "Coach Office, York" — describing the box & desiring [him] to look for [it] & send it back as soon as possible ... Met Captain Priestley who walked up with me to the White Lion to see the guard [of the mail coach]. Gave him my letter to the proprietor & promised 2/6 if he would see that the box was brought back safe & sound, as the guard who took it on Friday will not be here again till Wednesday (I believe the same guard goes thro' to Edinburgh) ... Walked to Sowerby bridge turnpike to inquire myself whether my box had been sent or not. Answer, yes.' [Journal entry 15.4.1820]

The next day ...

'To my great comfort & satisfaction Thomas (my aunt Lister's servant) brought me my box, quite safe, at 7, it having come from York by the mail.' [Journal entry 16.4.1820]

Anne's relief, after three days of worry and agitation about her box, was palpable. Once the journal had been retrieved she began to catch up on the entries she had been unable to write during the temporary loss of the box. She had a full seven days to catch up on.

> *'Wrote out my journal from 10 April.'* [Journal entry 17.4.1820]

--- Natasha's diary in the age of technology ---

Tuesday 27th September 1988, Home

Went to the library. Photocopied twenty-four pages of this school diary in case I lose it (£2.40. Bargain).

Wednesday 23rd January 2008

Stayed at work using a scanner with automatic document feeder that the workstation guys had furtively set up for me (without Les the purchasing guy finding out). Wanted to scan in all the photocopies of my old diaries from the early 90s. Hundreds of pages, maybe a couple of thousand. N. had done some with me at her work last term. Assumed I'd be up all night. Had a bit of speed in my pocket (I tend to carry it around just in case). [...] I left around 4:40am.

Thursday 31st January 2008

Bottle of vodka to N. to say thank you for spending hours of her Sunday at her office helping me to scan in my diaries.

ଚ୍ଚର୍ୟ
The mentality behind keeping a detailed diary

Natasha

Over the years I have caused my friends and family some annoyance by being unavailable to them, whilst in the same physical space, as I sat and wrote for hours at a time. I believe Anne was quite secretive about her record-keeping, whereas I was quite brazen?

Helena

Anne was not really so secretive about her journal. Granted she mostly wrote it up in the privacy of her bedroom, whether at home or abroad, but she would occasionally leave it lying around for others to see, confident in the knowledge that no-one could decipher the coded passages.

On occasions, when in Paris, she read aloud to Maria Barlow some entries from her journal, although she altered some of it as she read to disguise some of the truths in it.

> *'In the evening, till 11-50, read aloud [to Mrs Barlow] from my journal from 1 Septr to 19 Octr last – disguised a little now & then but not much. Barely enough to make it go down with her at all.*

She wishes to have all the rest up to the present. I must indeed begin to alter more by & by & she certainly would not like all my reflections. Poor soul. She does not know me quite. She has often said any woman might take me in.' [Journal entry 27.1.1825]

'Read aloud my journal of October 26. Mrs B[arlow] annoyed that I would not read her that part about M. Chateauvillard [a guest at 24 Place Vendôme, Paris, who had spread rumours about Mrs Barlow's affairs with men]. I had given Madame de Boyve [the proprietress of 24 Place Vendôme, who had told Anne about the rumours] my honour I would never mention [it] & therefore I would not do it.' [Journal entry 3.3.1825]

The friends in her Halifax social circle were fully aware of her journals. When Isabella Norcliffe was visiting Anne at Shibden they called on a Halifax family, the Saltmarshes, and Isabella spoke of the journals.

'Isabella, much to my annoyance, mentioned my keeping a journal & setting down everyone's conversation in my peculiar handwriting (what I call crypthand). I mentioned the almost impossibility of its being deciphered & the facility with which I wrote & not at all shewing [sic] my

vexation at Isabella's folly in naming the thing.'
[Journal entry 16.8.1819]

Needless to say, the gossipy grapevine of a small provincial town soon ensured that the news of Anne's journal-keeping became common knowledge amongst the rest of her friends.

So, people were wary of Anne's journalising. At one point Anne lamented to her friend, Mrs Waterhouse, that her friendships within her Halifax social circle were not the same as of old. Of Mrs Waterhouse's response, Anne later wrote:

'It was my journal that frightened people. She had made up her mind not to open her lips before me. Mrs Rawson, at the Saltmarshes', had abused my poor journal — wished I would destroy it — it reminded me of a great deal I had better forget.'
[Journal entry 25.3.1824]

Anne's motives for keeping such a detailed record of her life are expressed in various quotes throughout her journal. For instance:

'I might exclaim with Virgil, In tenui labor, but I am resolved not to let my life pass without some private memorial that I may hereafter read, perhaps with a smile, when Time has frozen up the

channel of those sentiments which flow so freely now.' [Journal entry 19.2.1819]

'I owe a good deal to this journal. By unburdening my mind on paper I feel, as it were, to get rid of it; it seems made over to a friend that hears it patiently, keeps it faithfully, and by never forgetting anything, is always ready to compare the past & present & thus to cheer & edify the future.' [Journal entry 22.6.1821]

What were your motives for keeping such a detailed record of *your* life?

Natasha

I have always been clear about my motives:

- I felt driven. I felt I didn't have a choice
- Fear of losing my life through forgetting
- Obsessiveness
- The realisation as a child that I loved reading back over my diary entries
- The joy of owning a record of my life
- The use of my diaries as reference books
- Historical interest
- Making money

Helena

The emotional and psychological significance of her diaries for Anne included:

- A desire to create a memorial of her life
- An aide-mémoire for her old age
- A record of her quest for self-identity
- To create a space in which she could explore her sexuality
- A confessional device (in the coded sections)
- A catalyst to relieve her emotional distress
- A therapeutic tool which helped her to make her way against all the odds, in a world which did not recognise, or was hostile to, the lesbian woman

If we agree with Philippe Lejeune, specialist in autobiography, in his work *On Diary*, that journals are 'an identity in process even as they are part of the process itself of creating identity, day after day,' then perhaps it is possible for us to try to understand, in Anne Lister's case at least, the mentality behind keeping such a voluminous and detailed account of her life.

Anne's journal, between the years 1806 and 1810, served mainly as an account of her day-to-day activities. The brevity of the opening sentence, 'Eliza left us', written on 11th August 1806 when Anne was fifteen years old, concealed a degree of unhappiness to which, at that time, she was unable to give full vent. It was only by developing a secret, esoteric code that she could create a private space in which she could not only chronicle her sexual life but also where she could explore and define her own nature.

On a more prosaic level, the journals served as a vehicle for (to quote Philippe Lejeune again) 'capturing the movement of time and the impact of daily experience' and also provided a 'record of a life process ... part of the practice of narrating and understanding what a life means.' But, more importantly, in Anne's case, they became, over the years, the recipient of her deepest emotional needs and crises. The use of the secret code in particular enabled her to engage in her quest to understand her own sexuality and achieve a sense of self which would enable her to operate fully in society for there were moments when her level of self-doubt about the validity of her own existence as a human being overwhelmed her.

The importance of Anne's journals in their role as her confessor and therapist cannot be overestimated.

Writing her journal became an emotional outlet and a psychological prop for Anne and, inadvertently, provided the foundation for a literary masterpiece which has now found its rightful place in the canon of other famous English diaries.

What were the emotional and psychological reasons inherent in diary-keeping for you?

Natasha

The emotional and psychological factors for me have been:

- Pride in my feat — both the enormous amount of work and the uniqueness of it
- The pointlessness of doing, thinking, or feeling anything if it weren't to be recorded
- Relief in capturing everything, of getting up-to-date in my recording
- Diary-writing is the most important aspect of my life
- Diary-writing is a tedious, time-consuming bind
- I have a love/hate relationship with diary-writing

--- Anne's mentality behind keeping --- a detailed diary

22.8.1823

Writing my journal has composed & done me good, so it always does.

16.9.1823

Writing my journal has amused & done me good. I seemed to have opened my heart to an old friend. I can tell my journal what I can tell none else.

31.5.1824

Sat down to my journal ... in the last 2½ hours, I have gradually written myself from moody melancholy to cheerful contentedness.

31.5.1824

What a comfort is this journal. I tell myself to myself & throw the burden on the book & feel relieved.

--- Natasha's mentality behind keeping --- a detailed diary

Wednesday 14th November 1990, Boulogne

Lay in bed reading *1984* by George Orwell. Felt frustration at how slowly my life is moving. Waiting to be free. I could drop out. I can't. My diary is mental stimulus at least. And listening to the Velvet Underground is a trip. Felt quite spaced out.

If I were robbed of my diaries, I'd be free because I'd no longer live. I want to die I want to die I don't even want to die I just want not to exist just no crap and no hassle and no hurt. I'd stop living and writing now if I believed no-one would ever read this.

Saturday 12th January 1991, Boulogne

Metro Burger for coffee and to write my diary. It scares me that I might stop writing it one day. Hour after hour after hour. I am envious of people who just live. They leave and arrive without looking at their watch, spend time without preparing to record it, have conversations without editing them in their mind, without repeating exact phrases so as not to forget, and without leaving once the backlog to be written up becomes too burdensome. I hate it so much and it is the most precious aspect of my life. I have to keep writing for Alex. Could she reject this too?

Saturday 8th December 1990, Boulogne

Alex's and my diaries belong to each other.

Friday 1st February 1991, Boulogne

She was talking in a frenzy. Then she calmed down and started on my cakes — at intervals going back to knock on the bathroom door. *"Are you coming out?"*

And to me: "There's more to life than finding exciting things to write in your diary … like staying out of prison, for example." And she left 12:04am. That was one of the best things she's ever said. And she was wrong.

Friday 31st May 1991, Boulogne

2:50am I took my diary and locked myself in the loos. They knocked on the door a few times to check I was OK.

Later René came to tell me that he wanted to go out with Ange (me too!). What were his chances? So that he would leave me alone to write, I told René that Ange loves him. Go ask her.

ℰℐℂℬ
Encoding

Natasha

I read in Anne's diary that she believed her code was close to unbreakable. How did she create a code that was so hard to crack? What was her formula? Anne and I were both fortunate enough to have studied the ancient Greek language, which gave us a ready and obvious base on which to form a code.

Helena

Anne used a mixture of Greek letters, symbols which she apparently devised herself, and numbers.

The idea of using an esoteric code appears to have had its roots in Anne's burgeoning knowledge of the Greek language. In November 1806 she began to date her entries, occasionally, in Greek. By 1808 she had introduced the rudiments of what was eventually to become an elaborate code, her 'crypthand,' as she called it, the use of which allowed her the freedom to describe her intimate life in great detail.

There are then tentative efforts to construct the odd sentence in symbols, some of which Anne herself apparently devised. A very early attempt at documenting her intimate life appears to deal with her menstrual cycle,

i.e. on Wednesday 6th December 1808 she writes, in code, *'Began very slightly.'*

Anne felt safe in the knowledge that no-one would ever be able to decipher the coded passages (in this, she was to be proved wrong) and as her confidence grew, the coded passages became longer and much more explicit when dealing with those aspects of her life which could not be written about in 'plainhand.'

I studied six languages at school, so when I wished to record the odd sentence that was supremely private, I first translated it into French or Italian, and then applied the code.

I generally didn't go to any great lengths to ensure I had an uncrackable code, however. Anne was not writing for an audience, but I was. I wanted my diaries to be read, to be published.

How many symbols did Anne use in her diaries?

Helena

Seven, so far as I can ascertain. They are as follows:

L	**indicates a letter received or sent**
N	**indicates a note received or sent**
c	**someone pays a social call on Anne**
√c	**Anne pays a call on someone**
@	**indicates a sexual session or 'kiss,' as she termed orgasm, with one or other of her lovers**
x or +	**usually indicates her autoerotic practices. Later we see this symbol followed by the phrase '*Incurred a cross last night*' (in code). Sometimes +, if not followed by *Incurred a cross* also indicates a reading session, as she usually confirms by naming the book in question**
§	**indicates certain key developments in Anne's relationships with women**

<u>Natasha</u>

I used the symbol 'X' to refer to Miss Williams, to further conceal who I was writing about. And in my early twenties I started marking at the beginning of each entry whether I had recorded a dream or received a letter. I used a flower for each. It was the position of the flower that indicated which had occurred — or two flowers for both.

How did you realise what the 'autoerotic' cross meant? Did Anne always write about this as well, or sometimes just use the symbol?

It was difficult to ascertain the exact date when Anne first began to use this symbol. The early indications seem to be in the latter half of 1816, when a small, insignificant ˣ began to appear in the margins of different entries, but as no comment or explanation for them was given it was not possible to be sure of their meaning.

Later, on 12th September 1818, she writes in her crypthand, *'Thinking of Miss B & just escaped +.'* From then on, at sporadic intervals and usually following bouts of erotic reading or fantasising, the crosses appeared in the margins of certain entries followed by the coded comment, *'Incurred a cross.'*

The quasi-religious and penitential nature of both the symbol and terminology signifies Anne's sense of religious guilt and she regularly prayed to God for the willpower to resist such sexual indulgences.

Did you ever teach your secret code to anyone?

Natasha

Yes, to just one person — to Alex, the young woman I met in Germany in 1989. Our romance is documented in my book *Lesbian Crushes and Bulimia: A Diary on How I Acquired my Eating Disorder*.

Alex and I wrote numerous romantic letters to each other in my code, safe from the prying eyes of our parents. This allowed us to express ourselves with complete freedom, of course. She started writing her own diary in my code, too. I like to think that she still uses it, twenty-seven years later.

Did Anne ever share her code?

<u>Helena</u>
Yes. Eliza and Mariana were the two people with whom she shared her code. There was also an instance of the construction of a consonant code which, I believe, she devised for communication between herself and a Miss Vallance, with whom she had a short affair when at Langton Hall — but there are only about two instances in the journals of her using this code.

--- Sample of Anne's code ---

--- Anne's 'crypthand' de-coder ---

'Number' codes

Code Symbol	Clear Text
1	k
2	a
3	e
4	i *or* j
5	o
6	u
7	y
8	w
9	z

'Letter' codes

Code Symbol	Clear Text
n	g
ŋ	gg
o	d
p	r
v	f
w	x
x	Mr
x̶	Mrs
x̄	Miss

'Greek' codes

Code Symbol	Clear Text
θ	v
⍵	h
φ	ff
δ	l
π *or* ×	and

'Bracket' codes

Code Symbol	Clear Text
(	b
⊢	bb
)	c
⊣	cc

'Line' codes

Code Symbol	Clear Text
—	m
\	n
⊼	nn
‖	q

'Arithmetic' codes

Code Symbol	Clear Text
+	p
=	s
‡	pp

'Tilde' codes

Code Symbol	Clear Text
~	t
✝	tt

'Punctuation' codes

Code Symbol	Clear Text
;	ee
:	ll
!	oo
?	ss

'Misc' codes

Code Symbol	Clear Text
▽	ch
^	sh
✓	th

A dot above a code symbol, or a code symbol underlined, denote repetition of the clear text

Guy Lawton, 2009

48

--- Sample of Natasha's code ---

--- Natasha's encoded diaries ---

--- Natasha's encoding ---

Saturday 12th August 1989, Germany

Alex had told me that she couldn't keep a proper detailed diary, because her mum has read it. I had suggested teaching her the Greek alphabet plus my own symbols, the code in which I write my own diary. She had sounded keen. I asked her tonight if she wanted to. She did. We sat in the Taverna. I wrote the rules and some examples in her notebook. I really enjoyed that. I showed her my diary and searched for a sample for her to decode.

Wednesday 13th March 1991, Boulogne

Jon asked if he could see my diary. He looked entranced as he turned the pages. He said, "This is really the weirdest thing I've seen in my entire life."

Thursday 2nd May 1991, Boulogne > Amsterdam

A guy came up and asked to see my diary. He studied the writing, said that it's like something from the middle ages. Ange said that she felt ever so proud to be sitting next to me.

Indexes

Natasha

In my early twenties I started adding a chronological index at the back of each of my diaries — a summary of what had happened each day. Later still, I added a further section that allowed me to add extra material that I had forgotten to record at the time. I was often writing as much as four thousand words per day, so these appendages added to the burden. Did Anne include an index in her diaries?

Helena

Anne constructed four different indexes beginning with a journal index in 1816, in which she recorded a short abstract of each day's entry in her main journal.

Over the next two or three years there emerged a literary index, in which she listed all the books, pamphlets, reviews, etc., which she had read or partly read throughout each year; a letters index which allowed her to track down the date, and the name of the sender or recipient of every letter during each year; and an extracts index listing the subject of each extract from her reading, alphabetically.

Her enthusiasm for keeping her indexes up to date eventually wavered and by 1830 she had virtually ceased

keeping these very time-consuming records, although at the same time her attention to her journals proper increased rather than diminished.

--- Sample of Anne's indexes ---

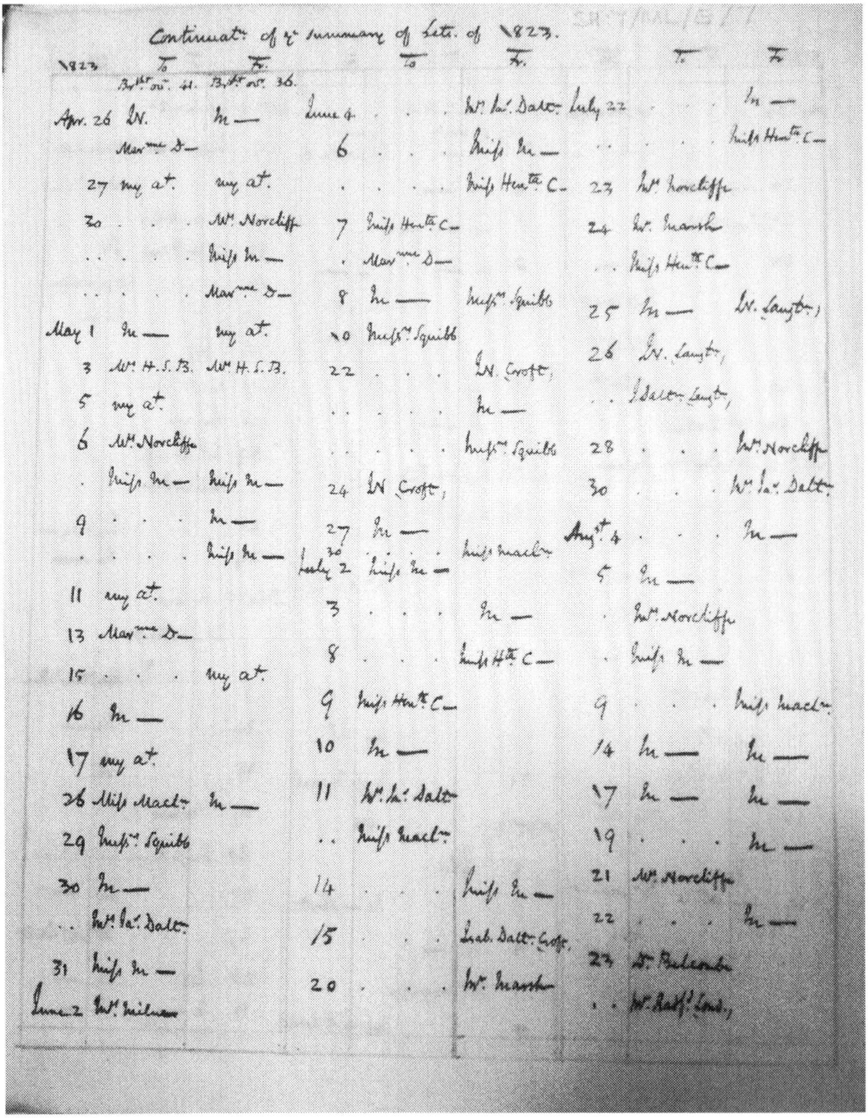

--- Sample of Natasha's indexes ---

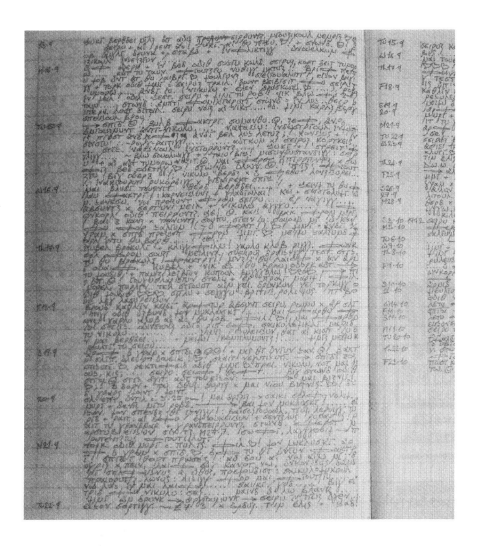

Similarities and differences in Anne's and Natasha's diaries

Natasha

What strikes you as the key similarities between Anne Lister's diaries and mine?

Helena

- **The most obvious similarity is the use of a secret code or script.**
- **The fact that within that secret script you both write so frankly about your sexual lives.**
- **The struggles you both encountered and described in constructing your own lesbian identities.**
- **The fact that you have both written literally millions of words.**
- **Your choices of strong hard-backed books in which to write your lives.**

Natasha

In what ways are Anne's diaries and mine most dissimilar?

Helena

- Anne's text is a mixture of coded and non-coded entries whereas you wrote entirely in code.

- Different techniques were employed in the devising of your codes. You each supplemented the Greek alphabet in different ways. Anne also added numbers, which you did not. You occasionally used other languages (French and Italian), which Anne did not.

- You did not utilise the margins of your entries in order to signify certain events as Anne did for both mundane events, such as sending or receiving a letter, and sexual activity signifying her autoerotic practices, and the levels of satisfaction in her lovemaking sessions with women.

- In your coded text you employed grammatical correctness in that you wrote complete sentences with full stops, commas, and spaces between words. Anne's coded passages run on without any grammatical input at all, so it has to be the decision of the decoder to impose a structure on the sequence of words that emerge — to define where words and sentences begin and end.

--- Anne's and Natasha's ---
approach to encoding

(Anne: part 'plainhand,' part code; Natasha: all code)

ℰℐℂℛ
Obsessiveness

Natasha

Did Anne write every detail of every day (which I have done continuously for periods of several years at a time)?

Helena

Anne wrote extremely comprehensive accounts of each day, even down to recording the times and duration of each of her activities.

Natasha

I see keeping a diary as an obsessive act. I'm aware that Anne and I are both obsessed too with making good use of time. Do you have a feel for Anne as an obsessive character in other ways?

Helena

Anne's obsessive nature is, of course, displayed mainly in her journal-keeping, as is yours, but it does manifest itself also in other ways, such as keeping a strict control over her finances. She had to have her accounts correct down to the last farthing (in pre-decimal currency, of course).

For example, on bringing her accounts up to date, she was gratified to find that they balanced ...

> *'to a farthing ... I am pleased that I have kept my accounts so correctly. It is a real satisfaction to me & must be the best safeguard against extravagance ... I will always make my income suffice my expences [sic] & something more.'* [Journal entry 27.4.1820]

This was an ideal which she had to abandon later when she became the ambitious mistress of the Shibden estate, intent on glorifying and Gothicizing the hitherto relatively modest medieval manor-house.

Her obsessive nature is also revealed in her indexes. Anne kept an index of all the key events of each day in abbreviated form. She recorded every letter she sent and received together with the dates and names of the recipients or senders. She also kept literary indexes of books, newspapers, magazines, etc., which she purchased or obtained from the library.

Apart from her journalizing, Anne's other main obsession was her programme of self-education. She would rise at dawn to put in some hours of reading classical texts and studying French and Latin before the practical concerns of the day took over.

Natasha

Although I feel mentally stable, self-aware, and well balanced, I do sometimes question my addiction to recording my life, and the two or more hours every day that I devote to it. Do you feel that Anne Lister's obsessiveness was in any way unhealthy?

Helena

Most dictionaries explain that obsessive behaviour can be:

- motivated by a persistent overriding idea or impulse, often associated with anxiety and mental illness, or
- applied to a person who is continually preoccupied with a particular activity.

Lejeune, the specialist in autobiography, asks in *On Diary*, 'Is journal-writing a neurotic or obsessive activity or an exercise in training or self-discipline?' Having worked through the whole of the 6,600 pages of Anne's journals, my conclusion is that Anne exhibited all three behaviours: neuroticism, obsessiveness, self-discipline.

Anne's neuroticism can be seen in her concern for her health, which began to figure prominently in her daily entries following the discovery that she had contracted a venereal infection from her married lover, Mariana Lawton. She gave explicit descriptions of her symptoms almost every day for a number of years and when the infection had run its course she began to obsess about her bowel movements.

Anne's obsessiveness is evident in the daily writing of her journal, no matter what circumstances prevailed, whether it was rough notes to be transferred to her journal proper later or to entries made on the day in the comfort of her own little study.

And, of course, Anne's scrupulous attention to her journal reveals her self-discipline.

--- Anne's obsessiveness ---

13.5.1817

[I] mean to turn my attention, eventually & principally, to natural philosophy. For the present I mean to devote my mornings, before breakfast, to Greek & afterwards, till dinner, to divide the time equally between Euclid & arithmetic ... when I shall recommence my long neglected algebra. I must read a page or two of French now & then when I can.

1.11.1817

Morning & afternoon making out an index to my journal.

21.1.1818

... from 10¾ till 2¾ adding up & arranging on a new plan my expenses of last year. i.e. classifying them under the following heads – Clothes, Hair-cutting, oil & brushes, washing, sundries, Postage, Parcels, Stationery, Books, music, Charity, Presents, servants, chair-hire, Travelling expenses, 2 courses of lectures, shoe bill at Hornby's of last year ... so that I can see at a glance what I have spent during the year in each department. I mean to pursue this plan in future &, to save myself all the trouble I have now had in having the items of the whole year to separate & class all at once, I shall do it as I go along, regularly every month.

22.12.1819

[After a marathon stint of writing about the time she spent in Paris]
I have learnt something during the time spent in writing it – at least
I have gained a valuable turn towards a habit of patient reference &
correction which, should I ever publish, may be of use to me.

--- Natasha's obsessiveness ---

Friday 14th October 1988, University

I asked him about Miss Williams's file.

He said he wasn't prepared to let me see personal info like that. "I think you've gone too far with this obsession. Quite frankly I think it's unhealthy."

He said I couldn't be right in the mind and I should wash it out of my hair, concentrate on my future, on my degree, and on my social life.

When I left his office I really felt like I just didn't care about anything.

Wednesday 14th November 1990, Boulogne

What I need to survive is to be obsessively, besottedly in love.

Monday 5th March 1990, University

Also took the opportunity to gather some info on calorie-controlled diets, though she doesn't approve of these as it can lead to dangerous obsession. — My favourite.

Sunday 25th March 1990, Home

I now feel that I should like to be about seven stone. Largely this is because I'm missing the obsessiveness of the extreme diet, the thrill of stepping onto the scales. I feel frustrated. I just want to go back to university and starve myself. If I have no-one to love, then: lose weight.

Saturday 31st March 1990, Home
Twenty-five minute lecture from my mother this morning about the perils of eating 400 calories a day. Psychologically it's dangerous, leading to obsession. And physically it can be disastrous. It can seriously unbalance the metabolism (It's true. I haven't had a period since Monday 11th December). She said people die, or eventually become grossly obese, because their bodies cease to function properly. You should lose weight slowly. No, I want people to notice. Mum said, "If it's drama you want, then you really *do* have a problem." Drama. Good word. Yeah, that's what I want.

Wednesday 9th May 1990, University
I used to think of my body as unfeminine and unattractive. And I used to think that people might think I might be gay because of my hefty physique. She said that I'm not severely underweight at the moment, which displeased me. But I should certainly not go below eight stone. My periods will not return if I go below eight stone, she said.

> "What's bulimia?"
> "It's throwing up after eating."
> "What's anorexia?"
> "It's eating the way you are now."
> "So, I have both of those?"
> "Yes, you do."

"But they are just factual terms, not illnesses?"

No, according to her they are abnormal obsessions and psychological illnesses. Medically my condition is termed 'eating disorder.' She told me I was foolish and said that no-one could help me, I could only help myself. But I wasn't about to "go away and think about it."

Saturday 12th January 1991, Boulogne

I've got a proper period. Disappointing. Period equals no weight loss. Felt so hungry that I wanted to cry with exhaustion. I forget how unbearable it is.

∞∞
How Anne managed her lesbian sexuality

Natasha

Did Anne ever express a wish that she were heterosexual?

Helena

In all the years I have been reading the Anne Lister journals I have not come across an overt statement from Anne that she wished she were heterosexual.

Sadly for Anne, she had her heart broken by the love of her life, Mariana, who chose the easier path of leading a conventional, heterosexual lifestyle. Nearly two centuries later you had a similar experience, didn't you?

Natasha

Yes. In 1989 Alex came out to her mother about our relationship. Her mother's reaction was appalling. She sent Alex to counselling to 'cure' her, and admitted to me that she didn't care about Alex's happiness, she just cared about not living with "the stigma of having a gay daughter." Alex reacted to this by trying to form relationships with men.

Did Anne assume that there were a large number of women and men who are not heterosexual?

Helena

Anne's awareness of homosexuality on a large scale rested on her readings of Classical literature which brought her the realisation that male homosexuality was regarded as normal amongst the ancient Greeks. She gave very little indication that she knew of any such practices on the same scale in her own era although she did mention a local married man, Sir Thomas Horton, whose homosexual activities were the subject of gossip in town. Anne disapproved of such conduct, saying that ...

> *'Sir T[homas] H[orton] was proved to be a perfect man by his having a child & it was infamous to be connected with both sexes.'* [Journal entry 13.11.1816]

Anne thought that homosexuals, male or female, had to be faithful to one sex, to be true to their natural inclination for their own sex, and then allowances could be made. Her lack of knowledge about the extent of female homosexuality was demonstrated when, in her friendship with Miss Pickford, she prised it out of her that she had a female lover.

'She was the character I had long wished to meet with, to clear up my doubts whether such a one existed nowadays.' [Journal entry 1.8.1823]

Anne was, of course, referring to Miss Pickford's sexuality. Her wonderment at this revelation …

'Are there more Miss Pickfords in the world than I have before thought of?' [Journal entry 5.8.1828]

… arose from her previously held belief that there was no other being who had the same degree of female masculinity as herself.

'I know my own heart & I know men. I am not made like any other I have seen. I dare believe myself to be different from any others who exist' [Journal entry 20.8.1823]

… was the credo she had adopted from Rousseau and this had sustained the idea of the uniqueness of her own sexual nature.

Natasha
Did Anne wonder how her "oddity," as she called it, came about?

Helena

Anne spent many hours in private, pondering the mystery of her own sexual nature. In June 1824 she wrote to one correspondent ...

> *'I am an enigma even to myself and do excite my own curiosity.'* [Calderdale Archives . Ref. SH: 7/ML/140. Letter from Anne Lister, Shibden Hall, to Sibbella MacLean, Coll, Tobermory, dated 21st June 1824]

She looked to literature and to science in her endeavours to unravel the 'enigma' of her sexual nature. Later in 1824, during a long, confidential talk with Maria Barlow in Paris, she tried to explain her sexual attraction towards women.

> *'[I] said, how it was all nature. Had it not been genuine the thing would have been different. [I] said I had thought much, studied anatomy, etc., but could not find it out. Could not understand myself. It was the effect of the mind. No exterior formation accounted for it.'* [Journal entry 13.11.1824]

Natasha

So, Anne had no lesbian role models? How did she know how to go about it?

<u>Helena</u>

There were no lesbian role models available to Anne when her sexually active life began in 1806. That year, at the age of fifteen, she was sent to the Manor boarding school in York. There she shared a room with Eliza Raine. Anne, no doubt fascinated by Eliza's air of exotic difference, quickly began to cultivate the young, Anglo-Indian heiress. The two became firm friends and, before long, lovers. They addressed each other as 'husband' and 'wife.'

As to how she knew how to go about it, there is no graphic description given in those early years (unlike later years) — so it can only be deduced that her natural instincts were sufficient instructors in initiating her into how to please women sexually.

<u>Natasha</u>

Did you gain an understanding of how Anne, Mariana, and Tib were so at ease with it all?

<u>Helena</u>

Yes. The more I read about the three of them — entered into their lives and got to know their personalities — the more I found myself understanding their uninhibited, almost carefree, and certainly guilt-free attitude to their woman-oriented sexual lives.

Their tacit acceptance of each other's rather different lesbian roles created a sort of relaxed atmosphere around the subject and enabled me to gain an insight into how this trio of women 'managed' each other, although it has to be noted that I only really have Anne Lister's interpretation of what went on between them.

Natasha

Did Anne's aunt and uncle ever have a clue about her sexual orientation?

<u>Helena</u>

Although ultimately unrealisable, the thought of an idyllic future with Mariana comforted and sustained Anne for a decade and a half. At one point, during those years, she even went so far as to confide her hopes to her uncle and aunt.

> *'Talking after supper to my uncle & aunt about M[ariana]. One thing led to another till I said plainly, in substance, that she would not have married if she or I had had good independent fortunes. That her having C[harles] was as much my doing as hers & that I hoped she would one day be in the Blue Room, that is, live with me. I said we both of us knew we could not live on air. Besides, I did not like her being in Petergate & had rather have her at Lawton than there. My uncle as usual said little or nothing but seemed well enough satisfied. My aunt talked, appearing not at all surprised, saying she always thought it a match of convenience.'* [Journal entry 27.6.1822]

This unruffled reaction of her uncle and aunt to Anne's future plans for herself and Mariana indicates the degree to which they understood the nature of their remarkable niece. Aunt Anne was, perhaps, less knowledgeable than her brother, yet both kept their own counsel on the matter and while tacitly accepting her difference, the subject of Anne's sexuality was never openly broached in the genteel,

reserved atmosphere of Shibden Hall.

Did your parents know about your sexuality?

<u>Natasha</u>

I didn't tell them directly, but the clues were overwhelming. For instance, I attached a poster-size photograph of Miss Williams to my ceiling above my bed in my bedroom at home so that she would be the last thing I saw at night and the first in the morning. And I had 'I LOVE MISS WILLIAMS' tattooed on my wrist. It would have been pretty neglectful parenting not to have picked up on evidence such as this.

--- How Anne managed her ---
lesbian sexuality

15.8.1816

Anne [Belcombe] sat by my bedside till 2. I talked about the feeling to which she gave rise. Lamented my fate. Said I should never marry. Could not like men – ought not to like women – at the same time apologizing for my inclination that way. By diverse arguments made out a pitiful story altogether & roused poor Anne's sympathy to tears.

8.11.1816

Anne [Belcombe] & I lay awake last night till 4 in the morning. I let her in to my penchant for the ladies. Expatiated on the nature of my feelings towards her & hers towards me. Told her that she ought not to deceive herself as to the nature of my sentiments & the strictness of my intentions towards her. I could feel the same in at least two more instances & named her sister Eliza as one, saying that I did not dislike her in my heart but rather admired her as a pretty girl. I asked Anne if she liked me the less for my candour, etc., etc. She said no., kissed me & proved by her manner that she did not.

4.10.1820

Rather agreeablizing to Eli [Belcombe] who looked pretty. I think Anne [Belcombe] observed my doing so with rather jealous eyes. She thinks me making up to Eli. Am certainly attentive to her but cautiously without any impropriety that could be laid hold of – yet my manners are certainly peculiar, not all masculine but rather softly gentleman-like. I know how to please girls.

✵ Adult sexuality

Natasha

Do you feel that Anne was a transgender man or a butch lesbian?

Helena

In my opinion, Anne would have been, in today's terminology, a 'stone butch' (although I believe that is now an outdated term). The best indication of this aspect of Anne's lesbianism lies in her distaste at Maria Barlow's attempt to take the initiative in their lovemaking, i.e.

> *'In getting out of bed, she suddenly touching my queer, I started back. "Ah," said she, "that is because you are a pucelle [virgin]. I must undo that. I can give you relief. I just do to you as you do to me." I liked not this & said she astonished me … This is womanizing me too much.'*
>
> **[Journal entry 19.3.1825, Paris. *No Priest But Love*, p.85. See also two essays, 'Stone Butch' by Nice Rodriguez and 'Untouchability and Vulnerability: Stone Butchness as Emotional Style' by Ann Cvetrovich in *Butch/Femme. Inside Lesbian Gender*, edited by Sally R. Munt. Published by Cassell, London, 1988]**

Natasha

I went to great trouble to avoid being thought of as masculine in any way, for example for 365 days at the age of seventeen I wore a skirt every day, without exception. This obsession with being viewed as feminine was one of the factors that led to my eating disorder. Anne doesn't seem to have an opinion on people commenting that she's a man. Did you get a sense of whether she was offended, amused, pleased?

Helena

It was a source of secret amusement for Anne if people thought she was manly. On her trip to Paris, she was asked to move to the men's area at customs. This, and other similar occasions, amused her.

What upset her, however, was when raucous, rough men in the town shouted obscenities at her or attempted to molest her.

Natasha

Although I was clearly gay, and identified as gay, I was quite curious sexually about men and I acted on that curiosity. Furthermore, I welcomed the sexual harassment I experienced at work in my early twenties — which was an indication of my low self-esteem, of course, a condition from which Anne did not seem to suffer.

Did Anne ever express in her diaries the slightest interest, either sexually or romantically, in men?

Helena

Absolutely not. Although one or two men did signal their desire to court her she made it quite clear that their attentions were not welcome. During a process of burning and burying her adolescent past, Anne clarified and confirmed her determination to live her life according to her nature.

'Burnt all Caroline Greenwood's foolish notes & Mr Montagu's farewell verses that no trace of any man's admiration may remain. It is not meet for me. I love & only love the fairer sex & thus beloved by them in turn, my heart revolts from any other love than theirs.' [Journal entry 29.1.1821]

Anne successfully seduced many women, and sought to seduce many more. She paid small courtesies to Miss Browne, for example, and made tongue-in-cheek remarks and sexual innuendoes, which went over Miss Browne's head.

What strategies did you use when you wanted to impress or flirt with a girl who may not have been aware of your sexuality?

Natasha

No doubt I was oblivious at the time, but it seems to me now that my behaviour twenty-plus years ago towards women I was attracted to was constructed precisely to avoid sexual contact.

I used to long for — and try to cultivate — intrigues where there was a strong element of yearning, of the forbidden. My ideal encounter was a mutual attraction in which we would have barely a hint that the other was gay and where we would need to tentatively draw this information out of the other — heroically combating social and religious mores — whilst falling in love. My burgeoning relationship with Alex fed into this pattern beautifully.

At my disposal for my tentative revelations I had my tattoo (which I could conceal beneath a watch, or partially expose), a dash of rainbow in my accessories, women's sign and labrys jewellery (how thrilling that I wouldn't know whether she knew what they meant).

I would introduce topics that were highly emotionally charged, drop subtle hints, engineer cryptic conversations, write ridiculously long letters about feelings. I would pay a great deal of attention to her, asking her abundant questions about her life, holding her gaze for just too long. I was intellectually arrogant, analysing her answers and showing off about it.

Everything had to be so deep and meaningful. If a woman had simply asked me on a date or asked me to sleep with her, I would have been utterly thrown.

Did Anne express any fears about getting caught?

Helena

On the whole, Anne was pretty confident that her sexual activities went undetected. The prevailing ethos of 'romantic friendship' provided a convenient cover for sexual behaviour between women in the privacy of their bedrooms and such was Anne's discretion and verbal dexterity that she was able to protect her 'veiled life' from those who took a more prurient view of her relationships with women.

Men, especially, were suspicious of her motives where women were concerned. In 1825, a York male acquaintance was heard to say he …

'would as soon turn a man loose in his house as me. As for Miss Norcliffe, two jacks together would not suit.' [Journal entry 12.9.1825]

--- Anne's adult sexuality ---

18.6.1824

[On looking over some of the volumes of her journal]

Volume three, that part containing the account of my intrigue with Anne Belcombe, I read over attentively, exclaiming to myself, "O, women, women!" I thought too of Miss Vallance who, by the way, is by no means worse than Anne, who took me on my own terms even more decidedly. The account, too, as merely noted in the index, of Miss Browne, amuses me. I am always taken with some girl or other. When shall I amend? Yet my taste improves.

22.7.1824

Two last night. M[ariana] spoke in the very act. "Ah," said she, "can you ever love anyone else?" She knows how to heighten the pleasure of our intercourse. She often murmurs, "Oh, how delicious," just at the very moment. All her kisses are good ones.

--- Natasha's young adult sexuality ---

Thursday 28th July 1988, Home

The conversation turned to Clause 28. John said teachers should be allowed to give an unbiased view of homosexuality because people think it's a disease. The other John said homosexuality is "demonic."
...

Friday 9th December 1988, University > Home

We left for the Vaults again about 10:40pm. Kate and Paulo walked ahead. Bogey and I stood in the High Street having the most passionate kiss. It was brilliant — delicious. I also got a love bite for the first time. We stayed there for ages. It was very hard to imagine it was Miss Williams because of his scratchy stubble.

Bogey and I eventually arrived at the Vaults 10:55pm and stood outside doing much of the same for five or ten minutes. It was great. I love Miss Williams.

Friday 30th December 1988, Home

There were a few of us in the back room. Dave Jarvis was washing his hands with liquid soap. He said to me, "Looks like spunk, doesn't it? ... Oh, you wouldn't know about that, would you?"

Saturday 6th May 1989, University

Went to The Halls disco. I was dancing with Ewan. At one point he went off and got himself a drink, but didn't offer me one. That does not impress me at all, but I wanted a kiss. His kiss wasn't excellent, but he certainly tried hard. His hands were up and down my back. He was kissing my neck — which I loved, and nibbling my ear — very nice. But I didn't enjoy the kiss. This time I remembered to imagine it was Miss Williams, but with his stubble, height, size, and sweat it didn't really work. He tried to invite himself back to my room for a coffee, but didn't succeed.

Friday 18th August 1989, Germany

We eventually had an open talk about our sexualities, which I managed to introduce. I told her that my only attraction towards men was one of sexual curiosity and the perfect thing would be sexual feeling with a woman. My emotional feelings are always towards women. I said, "I prefer women's faces." Alex said, "I do too."

She sort of agreed with me, but she always says she's confused. She knows that it's always women that she falls for, but maybe one day she'll feel the same for a man. She only wants this because she feels it would make life easier.

Friday 8th September 1989, Home

We took a taxi back to Louise's 1am. When we got in I asked her if she wanted a coffee, mainly because there was a room with a double bed waiting upstairs and I hadn't mentioned it and I felt rather awkward and embarrassed about it. We sat talking in the kitchen till 3am.

Saturday 9th September 1989, Home

I told her about my wanting the first bloke I sleep with to be someone significant and my consequently having propositioned my lecturer, Mr. Martin.

Friday 20th October 1989, University

Talked to Vikki. I really like her. She told me that she'd been in The Halls in her first year, but had had to leave in April because groups of boys used to shout "lesbian" at her and laugh when she walked into the dining hall. They used to urinate up her window. Incredible.

She has a much older girlfriend called Sam. Damn. I hate that. They all seem to have girlfriends. I hate couples. I like people to be available. One other girl and I were the only ones who did not look like stereotypical lesbians.

Tuesday 9th January 1990, University

Back to work 5pm. Cirio was as bad as ever. He was talking about sex as usual, got an erection, and physically forced my hand down to feel it. I've decided to reduce my hours to just Tuesday and Saturday.

Wednesday 31st January 1990, University

I hate sex. So bloody repetitive, and not a grain of emotion. Next, the penetration. It still hurt. I'd forgotten this. It feels like something's about to tear. I obtained absolutely no pleasure whatever from this. He then lay on his back and I sat on him. I couldn't even feel the intrusion.

Wednesday 12th December 1990, Boulogne

We were sitting close. Ange is one of those people who shies away from all physical contact that isn't heterosexual or parental. She hates the French custom of kissing on both cheeks and often refuses to do it with Didier and co. Now she said to me, *"On se fait la bise."* ("Let's kiss on the cheek.") She kissed me! She came towards me gently, in a way that was strikingly feminine. She kissed me on the left cheek. Then, kissing me softly on the right, the corners of our lips touched. ... She was doing this slowly enough for me really to sense that she was there, with me, she and I together, slowly enough for me to imagine. If it were really happening, it would have been amongst the most beautiful moments of my life.

Friday 11th January 1991, Boulogne

They were talking about how easy it is to get a French girl. Steve said, "You only have to say 'My bollocks are full, would you empty them for me?'" I hate heterosexuality so much. I can't even understand it. It's not love, it's hatred. A man on the hunt for a body to fuck. And it claims to be the superior sexuality?

Sunday 20th January 1991, Boulogne

Walking back, we saw a girl he knew. I asked him about her. She was a one-night stand from a disco. She danced with him and kissed him. She wanted to have sex. It was 4:30am, so they found a dark alley.

"Did you think less of her for it?"

"Yes."

I pointed out that they were two people who had done exactly the same thing. He gave me some crap that it lowers a girl and not a boy. So, it was he who lowered her then? I hate that so much. It's so obviously untrue.

Wednesday 27th March 1991, Boulogne

I shouldn't feel bad about so wanting physical contact. Everybody does. Woman to woman. The idea is so sexually exciting to me.

Friday 24th May 1991, Boulogne

I hate Ange for her heterosexuality and for her teasing me more often than I can even record, incessant reminders of what I can't have with every girl I want.

℘ Christianity

Natasha

Because of the fear of the afterlife, instilled in me from my religious upbringing, I was a Christian for a few years as a teenager, which stifled the expression of my sexuality for some time. How did Anne reconcile her sexuality with her Christianity?

Helena

Throughout her adult life, Anne never experienced any difficulty in reconciling her lesbian sexuality with her Christianity. Her firm belief was that as God had endowed her with her sexual nature it would be wrong to act against it.

Although Anne was unconventional in her candid pursuit of women and enjoyed the fact that people found her eccentric, she was an upstanding citizen with regard to her Christian religion and to living within the law.

Natasha

I enjoyed wearing both 'upstanding' and 'eccentric' hats, too. I was a model student, putting so much time and energy into my studies. But I loved being seen as 'weird' or unconventional in any way (anything that would serve to attract Miss Williams's attention, in fact). Unlike Anne, of course, I later veered into petty crime, getting quite heavily into shoplifting and drug-taking.

Did Anne ever consider her sexuality or extra-marital sex to be sinful?

Helena
As I state above, Anne considered her sexuality as God-given, natural and therefore not sinful. When Mariana's sister, Anne Belcombe, whom Anne was attempting to seduce, asked whether sex between women was wrong, whether it was forbidden in the Bible, Anne defended herself by pointing out that it was male homosexuality which was ...

> ***'positively forbidden and signally punished in the Bible. That the other [sex between women] was certainly not named.'* [Journal entry 13.11.1816]**

Anne's lack of conscience in her relationship with Mariana in particular arose from a sense of her natural right, by virtue of their deep commitment to each other prior to Mariana's marriage to Charles Lawton, to claim Mariana as her wife. In Anne's eyes, the sin of adultery lay in Mariana's union with Charles.

Her sexual affairs with other women did smite her conscience, not on a religious basis, but rather on the fact that she was being unfaithful to Mariana, her wife, e.g.

after contemplating seducing a young woman of her acquaintance she felt some remorse:

> *'How shockingly foolish I am. I really will amend. I now begin to feel I owe it to M-'* [Journal entry 21.10.1823]

Her real sense of sinning against God arose from her masturbatory practices. Anne struggled with her conscience when erotic reading or late night sexual fantasising about one or other of her lovers led to what she described as 'self-pollution,' about which she had an overwhelming sense of sinfulness. She regularly prayed to God for the willpower to resist such sexual indulgences but, as she wrote on one occasion:

> *'How frail is nature. How weak are all our purposes. 'Twas only last night, just before going to sleep, that I prayed fervently for God's assistance in all things. Oh, what a falling-off in me this morning. I have no confidence in myself, no strength to help myself — but I will not despair. I will yet pray & try, I hope with better success, to amend. Lord have mercy on me, a sinner.'* [Journal entry 13.1.1819]

--- Anne's approach to Christianity ---

29.6.1824

Mrs P[riestley] thinks me too light on religious &, perhaps, other subjects. Miss Hudson asked me if Mr Knight [the Halifax vicar] had ever talked to me on the subject. "Oh, no," said I. "He knows I would fly off at a tangent."

30.3.1823

Having gone to the new church did not stay the sacrament either today or Friday ... Felt remorse at not having fulfilled the Sacrament & afterwards, in bed, at night, prayed to be pardoned.

26.1.1826

[On the day of her Uncle James's death Anne was conscience-stricken to find that her main reaction was that of relief to find that she was now the rightful owner of Shibden Hall and its estates] I looked into my heart & said, Lord, I am a sinner. There is not that sorrow there ought to be. Felt frightened to think I could think, at such a moment, of temporal gains – that I was now sure of the estate. "Are others," said I, "thus wicked" and knelt down & said my prayers ... There is not that deep grief at my heart I think there ought to be. Oh, that I were better. Lord have mercy on me & forsake me not. Oh, cleanse my heart & forsake me not for mine iniquity.

--- Natasha's approach to Christianity ---

Saturday 8th September 1984, Home

UPDATE: I feel just awful when I read all those things back there.

I threw my fags away ages ago.

I do not intend to go out with any non-Christian boys, and I do not drink anything but cider and wine occasionally. Phew. THAT'S BETTER.

Sunday 3rd April 1988, France

In the night I needed the loo. It's downstairs, so I weed in my soap box. It went all over the floor. I threw what I did manage to catch out of the window. Thought there was grass outside. There wasn't. There's now a stain the size of a manhole on the concrete directly below my window. I was really frightened. Began to pray earnestly for rain. Prayed on Jesus's name for a miracle.

Three hours later, after I'd been asleep, I heard a curious scrubbing sound — my band of angels dancing on the spot with sandpaper shoes, I thought. The scrubbing sound went on a long time directly outside my window. I was too tired to get up and look, but eventually I did. The stain had gone. You cannot imagine my joy.

And in the morning I found out that it had rained during the night. Wow. ... I felt an incredible sense of nearly believing in Christianity. Discovered also that this was at the back of the house, where they never go. Jesus even turned the house round for me.

Monday 3rd October 1988, University

When I got back, the Christian Union had put leaflets under everyone's door. The girl in room 7 asked me if I was a Christian.

"... No." Bit sad, eh? First denial.

Sunday 4th December 1988, Home > University

Dad drove me to the station. We sat in the waiting room. ... And up came the long-feared subject: "Are you going to the Christian Union this week?"

I dread that so much. It makes me feel awful. "No."

"Please. For me?"

"No."

"It upsets me, you know." He was pleading with me. He looked like he was going to cry.

Tuesday 7th February 1989, University

At lunchtime in the Charleston Building foyer the Christian Union sang and gave talks. It was really good — especially looking at Hannah.

Thursday 2nd March 1989, University

7:30pm went to the Christian discussion group. Hannah wasn't there! Three people were leading it. And I was the only one who turned up.

Friday 5th May 1989, University

Went to the Christian Union meeting that Hannah invited me to. Hannah was leading it, so I could just sit and look at her.

Friday 9th March 1990, University

I resorted to amusing myself by asking her what her views were on a letter which appeared in the student newspaper today. It was an attack on homosexuality, legally and morally, and then condemned lesbian and gay Christians as hypocrites. I whole-heartedly agree. She'd only heard about the letter and I was unable to extract any personal opinions from her as we were being continually interrupted.

Later I walked back with Hannah and a girl called Anna. I was asking about themes of past Christian Union meetings. Hannah was quite surprised at my biblical knowledge. She joked that I probably knew more than she did. I've never told her I used to be a Christian. Amusing not to.

Hannah left, so I tried asking Anna. She indeed had read the letter. She was very reserved. She didn't appreciate my questioning. She said, "I feel like I'm on *Mastermind*." She said, "You're direct, aren't you." We agreed that Christian homosexuality was unjustifiable. I asked what a gay Christian should do. She looked *so* remote from the subject. She said, with complete incomprehension and an odd sort of 'kind' repulsion, "I'm told it's a feeling that you can't help." What an unbelievable lack of understanding. I asked her, "Have you never felt even a whisker of attraction to another woman?" She was shocked. She assured me that she had not.

Tuesday 2nd April 1991, Boulogne

Read Ensign, the Mormon magazine. On homosexuality it said that growing numbers of people are campaigning to make perverted acts between consenting adults legal and morally acceptable, attempting to prove that these impulses are inborn and cannot be overcome.

Friday 4th January 1991, Home

On the drive home, Dad said to me that he feels he's failed Louise. The night that Louise walked out to go and live with Nigel she told him that she wanted someone to love and look after her. Dad feels that if he had provided a better home life, she would not have needed to leave. He said that his relationship with our mother is the cause, and that had Mum not forbidden him to go to church and to take us to church (about ten years ago), then none of this would have happened. Dad and I both see Mum as a very unhappy woman. She shouts, moans, swears, and hates people.

Dad was telling me that he leads the Christian group at work Monday lunchtimes, attends some group at a church Tuesday lunchtimes, and something else still on Wednesday.

So, I challenged him: "Why don't you show it at home? One of the Christian teachings is that the man should be head of the household, and you let Mum walk all over you."

"I know you think that. You're always telling me."

I said, "It's no good being a closet Christian in your lunch hour."

Saturday 20th October 1990, Boulogne

Ange, along with the majority of the world's population, lives to be happy, with no belief in the afterlife. She said there's a whole world to be experienced, we can do and be what we want. I said that's barely true at all. Physically we are encumbered, in relationships we are dependent on the other person's feelings for us. Barriers everywhere. I told her that if I didn't fear what I would meet on the other side, I wouldn't be here now.

Saturday 12th January 1991, Boulogne

Huang believes that "good people" will go to Heaven. I explained to no avail that this is bullshit. That's not what the Bible says. His company was numbing me.

Tuesday 12th February 1991, Boulogne

Why bother living and why bother writing all this down when I am just waiting to be damned?

Friday 15th February 1991, Boulogne

He asked me why I'm not Christian. I replied that there are too many holes. How could an all-knowing God write as his word a book that can be so twisted and misinterpreted? He couldn't answer me.

Sunday 7th April 1991, Boulogne

Didn't get a wink of sleep, thinking about whether Mormonism is true.

Ange arrived 8am. I explained that I might fall asleep in church. She frowned. "You haven't had a reply to the prayer?"

I indicated the cigarette that I was smoking. "No."

Tuesday 9th April 1991, Boulogne

She told me of a Christian couple they know who were due a visit from the Mormons. The couple prayed beforehand to *bind* the Mormons' spirits. The Mormons told the Christian couple that they felt no Spirit that evening, and they never came back.

According to Mrs. Gage, she and her husband are on the Mormon blacklist of people they are forbidden to visit.

She asked if she could pray for me?

Yes, I'd really like that.

She meant *now.* ... "Do you mind if I lay my hands on you?"

I liked the idea of a woman putting her hands on me. "No, not at all."

She placed her left hand on my right shoulder, and her right hand above my chest. We both had our eyes open. She was looking at me. And I was looking into the air.

Her prayer alternated between English words and whispered speaking in tongues. She was asking the Lord Jesus to demonstrate the true path to me. I was listening intently to make out the sound of the tongues. ...

"Lumi blah blah ..."

೫ℭ३
Personal development

<u>Natasha</u>

I was brought up in a right-wing, Christian, middle-class environment. The political and social naivety of my early years pains me to read back over. I'm aware that Anne was solidly classist. But have you found her to come across as feminist in any way in her diaries?

<u>Helena</u>

Anne, unfortunately, was not a feminist. She opposed, rather than supported, higher education for women.

> *'I spoke against a classical education for ladies in general. It did no good if not pursued & if [it was] undrew a curtain better for them not to peep behind.'* [Journal entry 20.9.1824]

Initially, she was outraged by the thought of giving women the vote. Reading a publication in the Manchester Observer by one James Wroe, which favoured the reformers and the rights of women, she dubbed it ...

> *'a most seditious rousing article ... what will not these demagogues advance, careless what*

absurdity or ruin they commit!' [Journal entry 6.12.1819]

However, some years later she did express her thoughts about giving women of a certain class (i.e. her own) the vote:

'Musing ... this morning on writing a work on women, to follow up a petition to Parliament for women, under proper restrictions, being allowed to vote. I have long thought of the latter & that they have in fact the right.' [Journal entry 10.4.1831]

Natasha

I can empathise with my younger self (the 'little shit' that I was) when I read back over the distress, confusion, and emotional pain I experienced in the late eighties and early nineties.

It pleases me to believe that I have ironed out the questionable behaviour and character of my youth — the stalking, unkindness, depression, political ignorance. I *have* retained my drive and obsessiveness, though directed at healthier pursuits.

Did Anne make any advancement in character and attitude over time? In what ways, if any, did she mature?

Helena

A wild child, a flirtatious and sexually aware teenager, and an irresponsible young woman who had a number of

sexual liaisons, Anne's early life was nothing if not colourful. As she grew up, the more serious side of her character manifested itself in study, devotion to her aunt and uncle with whom she lived from 1815 onwards, and pride in Shibden, the ancestral home of the Lister family.

In 1816, when she was twenty-five years old, the disillusionment she suffered when the great love of her life, Mariana Belcombe, married Charles Lawton, brought a bitterness from which she never really recovered. She became more rakish in her sexual life. When her friend, Miss Pickford, asked *'Does your conscience never smite you?'* Anne answered ...

> *'No, it does not. But I mean to amend at five & thirty & retire with credit. I shall have a good fling before then. Four years. And in the meantime I shall make my avenae communes, my wild oats common. I shall domiciliate then.'* [Journal entry 30.8.1823]

In 1826 her uncle died and Anne inherited the Shibden estate. Coincidentally, that was the year in which she reached thirty-five — so her promise to 'domiciliate' became a very serious reality. As a landowner and woman of some consequence in the area, Anne knew she had to uphold the dignity of her position. In her journey toward maturity she had finally reached her destination.

--- Anne's personal development ---

2.9.1817

Spent the whole of the morning in vamping up a pair of old black chamois shoes & getting my things ready to go & drink tea at Cliff-hill ... Went in black silk, the 1st time to an evening visit. I have entered upon my plan of always wearing black.

7.6.1818

[Following an incident in which Anne felt snubbed by the Halifax socialites]

[I] shall make myself scarce to everyone. Determined to devote myself solely to study and the acquirement of that literature which may make me eminent and more decidedly above them all hereafter ... My mind was intent on these reflections as I walked along and I resolved to stick diligently to my watchword – discretion, & next to good, devote myself to study.

30.6.1818

Mused upon the practicability of aiding my classical studies under the tuition of Dr Carey. I should like to be at least six months with him. I 1st thought of this some time ago – soon after I began to study his elements of Latin prosody.

23.9.1825

Without some intellectual superiority over the common mass of those I meet with, what am I? *Pejus quam nihil* [a thing worse than nothing].

--- Natasha's then absence of --- personal development

Thursday 15th November 1990, Boulogne

The less I eat the sooner I'm out of here. I'd have to lose two stone to start looking obviously ill and I don't have the time before Christmas. I never had fainting fits. I'll need to do that. ... Dehydration? No, that was excruciating (Friday 4th May). Fake a collapse? Loss of employment for stonedness sits comfortably within cool. Consequences don't bother me.

Monday 17th December 1990, Boulogne

Walking across the playground, someone approached me from behind and called "Natasha." ... Céleste. She said to me, "Would you like to drink ... beer in a glass ... with me ... on Wednesday?" ... is what she said.

I replied, "I'd love to."

She suggested The Woolpack.

"I know it."

This girl is fourteen or fifteen. She's too young to be going out drinking. She said 2pm. That seemed a little flat. I'd assumed the evening.

I said, "... Thank you!" still rather surprised, and she turned and went back towards the school. Pupil-teacher relationships. What a fairytale. But she's not gay. No-one's gay. She likes me or she wants to practise her English. And if she's gay and she's falling in love with me, then good luck to her if she's got the balls to do it.

Thursday 18th April 1991, Boulogne

She was looking at a notebook of mine. ... Shit! She was on a page where I'd signed her name over and over when I'd had the idea of stealing her chequebook. On that same page I had written her cashpoint card number.

She asked why I had written her name.

"... I wondered what your name would look like in my signature."

She accepted that.

It was 5:49am. "Ange, let's go to a café on the port?"

She jumped out of bed.

I asked her, "Did you not notice anything strange in my notebook?"

"No. What?"

"Nothing."

"What?"

"It's nothing."

"You always do that. I *hate* it when you do that."

I showed her the page.

"You've written my card number down. Why?"

I was grinning. I wouldn't tell her.

She was guessing. "You're going to steal my chequebook?" She was joking.

I was grinning.

"Will you tell me?"

I was grinning wickedly. "Yeah."

"You were going to steal my chequebook?" She was looking seriously hurt. And sad. And calm.

I was being evil and loving it. Cold, controlled power. "Where do you keep it?"

"In the cupboard in my bedroom. ... I don't believe you."

"I don't lie."

"You wouldn't do that. You're my friend."

I was lying on my bed, grinning and enjoying this so much.

There were tears in her eyes. ... I held onto the moment. She would cry. And then I could hold her. That was my fantasy.

I explained how it would work. She didn't appreciate my cruelty. She said that I'd seen she was upset and I'd continued.

I said it was *good*. It was *emotion*. "I've never seen you show me so much emotion before. I wanted it to last."

Sunday 19th May 1991, Rouen

Into McDonald's for a Diet Coke. Ange joked about 'fancying' some guy in there more than me. I told her I didn't appreciate her saying things like that.

We went to the amusements and played *babyfoot*. I won all eight games. Two blokes wanted to play with us. One was very good-looking. Ange is rather pathetic in this situation — blushing and fumbling. They won.

The good-looking one started simulating sex with Ange, asking her if she'd like to make love with him. We said that boys don't approach girls like that in England.

Complete arseholes. Being gay *is* superior.

Back in McDonald's I felt cruel. I said that "girls with no hair" (as Ange calls women who think men are oppressors) are right,

and not to laugh at them. She said she didn't want to start an
argument with me.

"Well, you can defend yourself, can't you?"

"I'm your friend, I don't want to argue."

"Well, I feel angry."

"Against who?"

"Against your kind. ... That was a great advert for it."

"What?"

"That boy you found worth blushing over."

She asked me for the keys to the hotel, and she disappeared.
I *love* being cruel. Fuck those normal people. Vikki's angry, and
Ange laughs at her. Eat shit.

Ange returned a while later and sat down. ... Her stern face
disturbed me. ...

She said, "Is this going to carry on all night?"

"What's that?"

"Us arguing."

"We're disagreeing."

"No, we're not. You insulted me."

"How?"

"By calling me 'one of them.'"

"Well, you are — one of those *normal* people."

"Why are you angry?"

"That joke you made. It was unnecessary."

"I'd make that joke to anyone. I fancy him more than any of
my friends, more than that bloke over there. I'm not going to change
what I say because you're gay. That's promoting prejudice."

"Well, you wouldn't make a fat joke to a fat person."

"Why are you being so nasty?"

"It's part of my personality."

"I thought you were my friend. You're hurting me."

Alex left me for those wankers. I said, "Why don't you *learn*? It's *pathetic.*"

"So, I should stop being heterosexual?"

"No. I know it's not your fault."

"Now, let's get this straight: I'm pathetic?"

"*It's* pathetic."

"But I'm one of them."

"You're just a representative."

She marched out 7pm.

ಞಚಚ
Helena's reaction to Anne's and Natasha's diaries

<u>Natasha</u>

Were you genuinely shocked by anything you read in Anne's diaries?

<u>Helena</u>

'Shocked' isn't the right word. When I was young I spent a year working as a student nurse in a large psychiatric hospital and witnessed all sorts of deviant, including sexual, behaviour. I also had two experiences, in my teens, of amorous approaches (today we would say being 'chatted up') from lesbians. Also, a young school friend of mine came out to me as a lesbian, so I wasn't shocked, but reading the coded parts of Anne's diaries took me much more deeply into a world of which I had had very little practical knowledge, apart from the above minor experiences, and so I had to assimilate lots of new information.

<u>Natasha</u>

Did anything in *my* diaries shock you?

Helena

The most explosive episodes, for me, in your diaries were those which described your sexual experiments with five different men. I realise that your rationale lay in the desire to find out your true sexuality — but the accounts of each encounter are very graphic — as, of course, were many of Anne Lister's descriptions of her (lesbian) sexual activities. Once again, the assumed safety of your codes gave you both the freedom to be so explicit.

Natasha

What is your favourite part of Anne's diaries?

Helena

This is quite a hard question to answer. The choices are numerous. The fact is that the already published extracts don't, of course, tell the whole story.

Since starting to write Anne's biography I have had to delve back as far as 1775 (Anne was born in 1791) with her father's involvement as a soldier in the American War of Independence. From then on, it was quite fascinating to unearth the whole of Anne's childhood and teenage years — especially her schoolgirl love-affair with Eliza Raine when they were both boarders at the Manor School in York. So I really enjoyed writing about those early years.

Having said that, I was gripped by the drama of her love-affair with Mariana Belcombe — and then by the

Parisian period and her seduction of Maria Barlow. But it isn't just the personal side of Anne's entries which fascinate. It is also the way in which she described in detail the context of her life — the social, economic, and political background against which she lived out her life. So, you can probably understand my dilemma in trying to choose a favourite part!

Natasha
What is your favourite part of *my* diaries?

Helena
Each of the three books which you have published from your extensive three-million word, coded diaries has a distinct tone and a very different setting, but I was really taken with *Lesbian Crushes at School: A Diary on Growing Up Gay in the Eighties*. It is a remarkable study of a young girl's budding sexuality which conveys a sexual innocence and, at the same time, a growing awareness of the passionate intensity of, at this stage of her life, feelings which could convulse her emotional life without quite knowing how to name, or speak about, such feelings.

I think this book can be placed in the 'rite of passage' tradition in which the transition from childhood to adolescence is negotiated through hitherto unawakened desires for another person. Your feelings for Miss Williams went far deeper than just the usual schoolgirl crush. They in fact became the lodestar by which all your future heterosexual and lesbian relationships were, perhaps subliminally, judged.

Natasha

Do you like Anne?

Helena

Yes! I know a lot of people don't, but I do. Despite the fact that in politics, religion, and class status, we are complete opposites, her heartbreaking love-story and the courageous way in which she faced all the difficulties she encountered in living as a lesbian in that particular era command my sympathy and admiration. I haven't had the same experiences, of course, but I feel I can empathise through my imagination and also because I have a lesbian daughter myself.

Natasha

I was quite an unpleasant person in my early twenties (bitter, like Anne, that my beloved had sought a heterosexual lifestyle, against her nature), and I lay that bare in my diaries. For instance, I recorded the pleasure I felt on my year abroad in France, causing pain to my best friend, enjoying watching her cry. Did you find that you disliked me, at points, as you read my diaries?

Helena

It was not really a case of disliking you — more a case of disliking some of your actions, such as the one you describe above. This has also been the case with my feelings towards Anne Lister as I have worked through her journals. You were both experiencing the same dilemma, that of rejection by women whom you loved and, as Anne wrote ...

> *'The heart knows its own bitterness.'* [Journal entry 20.8.1823]

I will add that I admire both you and Anne for your courage in facing up to a difficult world despite the problems posed by being forced to 'go against the grain' of that world by your sexuality. As Anne Lister wrote ...

> *'Alas! I am, as it were, neither man nor woman in society. How shall I manage?'* [Journal entry 26.1.1830]

But manage she did, as you are doing, and, whatever her faults, her achievements as her life progressed marked her out as a woman of great abilities and fearless courage.

Natasha

Did any of the material from Anne's diaries work up any strong emotions in you?

Helena

Yes. Quite a lot of it, actually, but a particular entry which Anne made in her journal on 20th August 1823, after Mariana had humiliated her, moved me to tears. It reads that, although Anne is disillusioned with Mariana, yet *'Love scorned to leave the ruin desolate; & Time & he have shaded it so sweetly, my heart still lingers in its old abiding place.'* I think that is the most poignant sentence I have ever read about a broken love-affair.

Natasha

Do you feel as if you know Anne? Would you recognise her personality if it were possible for you to meet her?

Helena

I have been reading Anne's journals and letters for the past three decades and I feel I have as complete an understanding of her personality as it is possible to have when one has lived with such an honest exposition of the most intimate thoughts, feelings and actions as Anne's. I have also constructed my own image of her physical appearance so, when I read and write about her, this image is with me all the time. Should the impossible really happen, then yes, I would recognise Anne Lister.

Natasha

You and I have enjoyed meeting up on a number of occasions now.
Do you recognise anything of my adult self from my 1983-1991
diaries?

Helena

**From what you have told me of your present life I know
that you continue to live what I would consider a 'semi-
bohemian' lifestyle — very much toned down from that
which you lived in your younger years. You give the
impression of still being a risk-taker, but not in an
unlawful way.**

**The bulimia from which you suffered as a young
person has left its mark on your physique, I think, as your
(enviably) slim frame attests.**

**I also think that you are still hyper-active /obsessive
up to a point — but again in good ways. You are an older,
more stabilised, still highly intellectual and (I hope)
happier version of the younger Natasha.**

--- Natasha's shocking experiment begins ---

Tuesday 3rd October 1989, University

A few months ago I had decided I wanted to have sex with five men, before having sex with a woman, to see what it was like.

Went to The Jeans Company where I had met a boy called Larry last term. He was working there and had asked me about my tattoo and had told me he was gay. I had asked him about sleeping with a woman. He said he never had done.

"Would you like to?"

"As an experience, yes."

"If I offered, would you accept?"

"Why, are you?"

This had been our conversation then. Over the summer holidays I decided that if I couldn't get one of the lecturers to be the first then I would go for Larry. He would be different because he was gay. I really like him. He's sweet. I went in and asked if he was around. He was downstairs. He's not much taller than me. Brown hair, brown eyes, lovely smile. He remembered me, my tattoo, and our conversation, but was embarrassed when I asked him to repeat it. He blushed a bit and said, "Are you propositioning me?"

❧ Publishing

At what point did it occur to you that Anne's diaries were publishable?

Helena

When I first conceived the idea of writing about Anne Lister, I had thought that she would make an interesting subject for publication in a historical journal. I had no idea of her sexual orientation. It was only when I began to transcribe the coded sections that I realised that there was a much more dramatic dimension to her life than merely that of mistress of a local landed estate.

As I read further into her journals and uncovered the extent of what was on offer, there was no doubt in my mind that this journal was a significant historical document and therefore publication became an inevitable end product of all the work I was putting into the project.

Natasha

I use a pseudonym. Names and places in my published diaries are removed, altered, and disguised. My family and friends have no idea that I have published details of my (and their) intimate life. What did you agonise over regarding publishing details of Anne's life?

Helena

Her more explicit sexual activities with her lovers and the details of the venereal infection which Mariana Lawton transmitted to her were the two areas which caused me the most conscience-searching about whether or not I should reveal such intensely private material.

Natasha

Did you find any of it cringeworthy or hard to read?

Helena

I think my answer above covers this issue. I do remember mentioning my reservations about those two areas of Anne's life to a male acquaintance some years ago. His laconic answer — that "history is fair game" — made me less inhibited about revealing the truths of Anne's life. I realised that if you are going to write serious history it must be as true as you can make it from the facts in your possession. What is the point of history if it is constantly sanitised by omission of the more brutal realities? The prettier versions of history in the Georgian era can be read about in Jane Austen's novels.

Natasha

Do you have a secret collection of too private or favourite unpublished entries?

Helena

I wouldn't go so far as to say I have a secret collection. There is obviously a moral dilemma concerning the fine line between writing an account of a person's love /sexual life which is acceptable and writing about it for reasons of excessive prurience. I hope that I have so far struck a reasonable balance in the two books so far that have been published.

Natasha

Are you planning on publishing some of the steamier parts of Anne's diaries? What would persuade you?

Helena

I will probably continue trying to achieve the balance outlined above. As the journals are now online in the *HistorytoHerstory* project, anyone interested enough can search for themselves. At this point I would like to say that the sexual material in Anne's journals can be classed as erotica rather than pornography. It was a matter, for me, of selecting some of the extracts which gave enough sexual detail to firmly establish her true lesbianism without being

over-repetitive, which would run the risk of becoming tedious.

Natasha
Your second book of Anne Lister's diaries, *No Priest But Love*, which covers her stay in Paris, from September 1824 to October 1826, contains rather more details of Anne's sex life than your first. Why is that?

Helena
In my first book, *I Know My Own Heart* (now reissued as *The Secret Diaries of Miss Anne Lister*), because a number of years of Anne's journals are missing, I had to start with the ones available, i.e. 1816/1817. By that date, Mariana (Anne's lover) was already married. Any detailed account of Anne's early courtship of her was lost to us.

In *No Priest But Love*, however, we are able to follow every move in the courtship and eventual seduction of Mrs Barlow.

The deeper answer is that this is an important contribution to the history of women's sexuality — especially of lesbian sexuality. Lesbians are entitled to their history, including the history of sexual activity between women, and *No Priest But Love* is a classic text on the subject. Anne's compelling urge to write graphic descriptions of her sexual activities with Mrs Barlow is, I believe, a form of pre-Freudian psychotherapy in that it

gave her obvious psychological relief to confide to her journal what she could not speak about — 'the love that dare not speak its name.'

Natasha

You have read my heavily *edited* diaries, not the originals — which would have been a laborious task, owing to their immense volume, repetitiveness, minute detail, and lack of flow. You read Anne's *unedited* diaries, of course. What material did you find least interesting — particularly with a view to publishing?

Helena

Anne's role as estate manager, perhaps, which she adopted with enthusiasm once she had inherited the estate in 1826. Although of great interest to economic historians, the minute detailing of her plans to improve the estate at that period and also later, when she was able to avail herself of Ann Walker's money, fills pages and pages of calculations and costs, etc. Her overall plans are interesting, but the minutiae can be hard to plough through for her biographer.

Natasha

Was there any non-sexual material that you felt was too private to publish?

Helena

No. All that was written in her plainhand, although fascinating in its detail of family life on a small estate and the social life of the Georgian era in a provincial northern town, held no secrets. The non-sexual material in her crypthand passages concerned money, dress, humiliating episodes and scandalous remarks about her friends and acquaintances. All this was publishable.

Natasha

How did you decide what to leave out?

Helena

The decisions I had to make were not easy. In order to produce a viable book out of the four-million word journals, I had to find a theme around which I could organise some of the material. I therefore decided to concentrate on the most emotionally dramatic years of her life, 1816-1824, during which her love-affair with Mariana Lawton, née Belcombe, is chronicled in detail.

Consequently, Anne's early life (1791-1816) had to be omitted as well as a lot of local history, mainly of interest to Halifax people perhaps. A great deal of domestic detail relating to the running of Shibden Hall and its surrounding estate had to be excluded because of the repetitive nature of the entries. These omissions, and many others, are rectified in the biography of Anne's life on which I am engaged at the present time.

Natasha
How did you decide what to leave in?

Helena

Obviously, the most startling and intriguing theme throughout the journals was that Anne Lister was a lesbian and she had written explicitly about her sexual activities with other women. This alone conferred a distinct and, as far as we know, unique dimension to this historical document.

However, Anne is not to be defined solely by her sexual orientation. Her self-education, her love of travel, her management of the Shibden estate, her social life, her friendships, her family life, and many other facets of her life had to be taken into consideration.

In my selection of extracts from her journals I tried to present a balanced picture of her life and personality throughout the period I had chosen to work on.

Natasha
Were the decisions hard?

Helena

Extremely hard! In her earlier journals, Anne Lister gives us a wonderful panorama of Georgian life in a small provincial town. Later, as she becomes a much-travelled woman of the world, we move with her into a greatly extended cosmopolitan society.

In addition, we are privy to the most intimate details of her love-affairs with women. The dilemma of deciding what is of paramount interest in all this fascinating material makes for a great deal of indecision (about what to put in) and regret (for what I have to leave out).

Were your decisions on what to leave in and what to leave out hard when editing *your* diaries for publication?

Natasha

Generally, no. I had the cover of a pseudonym. But there are several parts that I left in that made me cringe at the time and still make me cringe when I re-read them. Of course, to the reader, these parts are likely to be the most entertaining. A diary *should* deliver raw information, it *should* expose its author.

I did initially consider, when working on the manuscript for *Lesbian Crushes and Bulimia: A Diary on How I Acquired my Eating Disorder*, whether I should leave out my whole sexual misadventure of experimenting with sex with men. Ultimately, I had to acknowledge that this was central to the story. I then had to decide just how much of the sordid, awkward, unsatisfactory experiences to include. As you're aware, I elected not to shy away from the facts.

The most painful section that I left in was Saturday 10th December 1988 in *Lesbian Crushes at School: A Diary on Growing Up Gay in the Eighties,* when I had to face Miss Williams with an apology for my dismal behaviour at the school Christmas Fair the week before. My complete lack of self-respect, and the utter futility of my behaviour towards Miss Williams, caused me to curl up and die afresh every time I redrafted and edited that manuscript, honing it into a publishable book.

Also, now, as a fully-fledged lesbian, I felt deeply irritated by including any attraction I used to have for men.

As for what I omitted ... I couldn't bear to publish a letter I wrote to Miss Williams after I left school.

I also omitted much creepy detail on my attraction to the idea of Jesus, my violent repulsion by the Bible, and my distress at needing to know whether Christianity was true.

What was your process for working out the continuity between the sections you left in?

<u>Helena</u>
When I first began working on the journals I found that I had uncovered two extremely fascinating themes: Anne Lister's intimate and complicated life as a lesbian in the Georgian era and a historical account of my own home town of Halifax as it was in Anne Lister's time, over two centuries before my birth.

It was thrilling to learn that Anne had walked the very streets which I had known all my life, that some of those streets were named after families she visited in her

time, that houses she visited were still in existence. This historical record of my town intrigued me and I was very tempted to include more and more detail relating to it. However, the Halifax Antiquarian Society possesses a wonderful archive of local history and I thought perhaps a book based solely on Anne Lister's Halifax would be superfluous and would perhaps appeal only to a limited readership.

In addition, Anne Lister's love for women and how she managed to act upon her sexual feelings for them was a much more universal theme than the parochial image of a small Yorkshire town, or even the much more sophisticated city of York, which she visited frequently, interesting though these two locations were.

My process then was to try and include in the linking passages between extracts as much as was possible to give a succinct account of the Halifax and York circles in which she moved and also summarise her activities at certain points to allow the progress of her love-affair with Mariana to move on.

What was your own process for ensuring continuity in your published diaries?

Natasha

I found continuity an interesting challenge because my diary entries are so lengthy. I couldn't remember, after twenty or thirty years, what information in earlier entries might become pertinent in later entries. To get it right, I had to read the material right the way through in a short space of time, so that I could hold all the threads of the stories in my mind.

Again for each draft I had to read the manuscript through in a short space of time to accurately tie up loose ends and remove anything that didn't make sense.

With my school diary, I drafted the manuscript four times before I felt happy that I had honed the book perfectly. My French diary took five times. I enjoyed the process.

<u>Helena</u>
Have you ever considered rewriting and publishing your diaries as memoirs or novels?

<u>Natasha</u>
Never. I love the brutally raw format of a diary. I don't want to deviate from that in any way.

--- Publishing Anne's diaries ---

The 1988 publication of an edited version of Anne Lister's journals, entitled, *I Know My Own Heart*, caused quite a stir, especially in the academic world, and drew comments from many writers and scholars in the field of women's history.

"The Lister diaries are the Dead Sea Scrolls of lesbian history; they changed everything."

Emma Donoghue

"Engaging, revealing, at times simply astonishing. Anne Lister's diaries are an indispensable read for anyone interested in the history of gender, sexuality, and the intimate lives of women."

Sarah Waters

"Anne Lister's sense of self, and self-awareness, is what makes her modern to us. She was a woman exercising conscious choice. She controlled her cash and her body. At a time when women had to marry, or be looked after by a male relative, and when all their property on marriage passed to their husband, Anne Lister not only dodged the traps of being female, she set up a liaison with another woman that enhanced her own wealth and left both of them free to live as they wished. ... The diaries gave me courage."

Jeanette Winterson

"Have no doubt; the [journals of Anne Lister] will be subject to international scholarly inquiry and analysis for generations to come, and they are an English national treasure."

Dr Catherine Euler, University of Arizona, 27.1.2011

"I feel that 'I Know My Own Heart' has been only the tip of the iceberg so far. The diaries need time to unfold in order to be appreciated to their full extent, and also to be allowed to make their full contribution to the canon of 19th century women's journals. I am sure they will eventually occupy a unique position in their genre simply because of their contribution to the understanding of women's sexuality in the 19th century."

Letter from Helena Whitbread to her editor at Virago Press, 1.3.1989

In 1992 a second volume of the Anne Lister diaries, *No Priest But Love,* was published. And in 2010 an updated and revised version of *I Know My Own Heart* was published by Virago with the new title of *The Secret Diaries of Miss Anne Lister.*

In 2011 Anne's journals were placed on the United Kingdom Memory of the World Register, part of Unesco's Memory of the World programme, a list of documentary heritage which holds cultural significance specific to the UK. The registration citation notes that it is the 'comprehensive and painfully honest account of lesbian life and reflections on her nature, however, which have made these diaries unique.'

--- Publishing Natasha's diaries ---

Friday 16th November 1990, Boulogne

Read *1984*. It's exciting. I want to write books that are episodes of my life.

Helena's experience
as Anne's editor and biographer

Natasha
What first drew you to Anne Lister's diaries? Was it a set project on your degree course or was it your own choice?

Helena
It was my choice. I had completed my degree course in Politics /Literature /History of Ideas at Bradford University followed by a PGCE course at Holly Bank Teacher Training College in Huddersfield and I had entered the teaching profession — mostly as a supply teacher (a conscious decision on my part because I really wanted to study and write), which meant that the work burden which full-time teachers have wasn't so heavy for me.

Thinking about a subject which could be researched locally, my mind turned towards Anne Lister as a historical person of some interest in my own town. I thought that I could perhaps write an article about her as a start to my idea of freelance writing. I knew that the local press had published some extracts from her letters in the past, but I knew nothing about a journal until the first day

I went to the Archive Department at Calderdale Library where her papers had been lodged since c.1933.

Natasha

Have you read all of Anne's diaries? How long did it take you?

Helena

I have read all of Anne's diaries. It took me four years. I began in 1983 when I first visited Calderdale Archives to enquire about researching Anne Lister. On that visit I obtained a copy of her code and then photocopied the first fifty pages of her journal to take home with me. Every week for the next four years I collected fifty pages to read and to transcribe the coded entries. There are 6,600 pages in total.

Natasha

What has been your favourite experience in the past three decades of your involvement with Anne's diaries?

Helena

The first five years of working on the journals before they were published must count as the best experience of my involvement with Anne Lister's journals. No-one (apart from my family and one or two trusted friends) really

knew about what I was doing. I had Anne Lister and her magnificently detailed life all to myself. It was more or less my secret and I loved the feeling of intimacy and the quiet hours of studying the life of this remarkable woman.

Once my first book, *I Know My Own Heart,* was published by Virago Press in 1988, I had to let go of that magical time and bow to the outside world. Although I have met a lot of interesting people and had many varied experiences connected to the publication of my books, including travelling on the Continent to speak at venues in various countries, the first five years were a never-to-be-recaptured idyll of quiet, scholarly work untroubled by the demands of the media.

Natasha

How has working on Anne's biography differed from working on her diaries? Which do you prefer?

Helena

The two distinctive approaches to the Anne Lister material, the editing of her journal and the writing a biography of her life, posed radically different problems.

When I first came across the Anne Lister journals I felt that I could, at that stage, only present the material in the form in which she had written it herself, that is, in diary form. Although she had lived, breathed and walked in and around my own home town some two hundred

years ago (and that was a great part of my delight in the work), the historical background of the wider canvas against which she lived her romantic and dramatic life, encompassing as it did practically the whole of the Romantic era, the French Revolution, the Napoleonic Wars, Restoration Paris, the rise of the Industrial Revolution, the British political scene in all its turbulence of those days, was so vast, so enthralling, that it overwhelmed me.

But here I had one, as yet unknown, voice of a woman, living in obscurity in a small Yorkshire town, whose journals could offer me a way into making that past come alive because her words provided a vivid day-by-day depiction of the extraordinary life she was living during that era. To quote from Stevens and Burg's useful book *Editing Historical Documents. A Handbook of Practice,* 'The authentic words of men and women from the past offer a way to experience the real thing ... they provide an immediacy not otherwise found in conventional narratives. [We are] reading the words of men and women who do not know how their own particular lives will play out.'

The problems lay, of course, in the difficulties posed by Anne's use of her esoteric code and her tiny handwriting, extreme use of abbreviations and sometimes the use of archaic words or phrases in her non-coded passages.

By the time I had worked through Anne Lister's entire journals (which included transcribing all her crypthand as well as her small, abbreviated plainhand passages), undertaken copious background reading into the era, and had written and published the two books of extracts from her journals, I then began to contemplate writing her biography.

But it took me a whole decade, from the publication of my second book, *No Priest But Love* in 1992, to pluck up the courage to start on the awesome task of writing the biography of Anne Lister. The problems thrown up by my decision to use the Lister documents in this very different form were daunting. Leon Edel, in his books *Writing Lives* and *Literary Biography,* enumerates four of the dilemmas which I have encountered (and I paraphrase his words a little here).

1. That of imposing order, bringing logic and shape to the record of someone's life.
2. How to marry the truth of life and the truth of experience when a biographer is outside his/her subject seeking to penetrate into the subject's mind, and obtain insights which are not vouchsafed him/her.
3. How to encompass all available data and yet reduce them to a manageable compass, to dimensions that can be comprehended by a biographer and an audience.
4. How to manage both sufficient immersion in the life of another to understand it, and yet enough detachment to analyse and explain.

To get back to your question of which of the two genres I prefer, they both have their intellectual attraction for me — but in the biography I do have greater freedom to expand on all the fascinating social, political and economic history of Anne's time, very little of which I could allow in the two books of extracts already published. So, I have to say that, because I can spread my (intellectual) wings, I find writing the biography perhaps more satisfying, albeit much more difficult, than the editing of her journals.

Natasha
Did any of Anne's revelations change your life?

Helena
I would not say that Anne's revelations changed my life. Whilst working on the journals I still continued my day-to-day routine of wife, mother, teacher, etc.

It was perhaps more the *publishing* of her revelations that changed my life. I found myself taken into quite a few different worlds — the lesbian world, the worlds of academe, publishing, film-making, travelling to cities such as Paris, Berlin, Bologna, and Zurich — to give talks about my work on Anne Lister.

As my then headmaster said, at the school at which I was working when my first book *I Know My Own Heart* came out in 1988, "You have lit a slow fuse." Very

perspicacious of him — the interest in Anne Lister and her journals has increased exponentially since that time.

Natasha
Did any of Anne's revelations change your view of human nature?

Helena
This is a difficult one to answer. I think that as we move through our lives our view of human nature does undergo change — life experience guarantees that. Only those of the most rigid, inflexible natures can remain unchanged by the world.

What I can perhaps say on this question is that after three decades of living and working with Anne Lister's journals I have developed a wider appreciation of the many diverse interpretations of female sexuality and a greater sense of empathy with the conflicts inherent in the realisation that one's sexuality runs counter to the norm.

Natasha
Did you know that Anne was a lesbian before you started on this project?

Helena
No, I had no idea.

What was your first clue that Anne was a lesbian?

Helena

Looking back, I'm not sure. The clues came out gradually. I did wonder, 'What is this woman hiding? Why does she need to use a code?' She expressed a lot of angst over what I initially saw as her 'friendship' with Mariana. It soon became pretty clear that her relationship with Mariana was at a much deeper level than 'friendship.'

The first hint that I uncovered did not emerge until May 1817. In a coded passage, Anne writes ...

> *'I begin to despair that M- [Mariana] & I will ever get together. Besides I sometimes fancy she will be worn out in the don's [Mariana's husband, Charles Lawton] service & perhaps I may do better.'*
> **[Journal entry 28.5.1817]**

From that point on the clues proliferated and it is possible to follow the trajectory of the disclosure of Anne's lesbian love for Mariana in *The Secret Diaries of Miss Anne Lister*.

When I first began to photocopy all the journal pages, the microfilm reels began on 17th March 1817. Much later, after Virago had published my first book *I Know My Own Heart* in 1988 (later expanded and reissued by them in 2010 as *The Secret Diaries of Miss Anne Lister*), I found

that there were earlier years which had not been placed on microfilm during my period of working on the journals, so I had missed some clues which would have led me to recognise her lesbianism much earlier.

Natasha
Can you describe the moment the penny dropped that Anne Lister was a lesbian?

Helena
I think the correct term for what I experienced is 'startled.' Whatever else I had thought I might find out about this intriguing woman, the fact that she was a lesbian had not even crossed my mind!

--- Helena's experience as Anne's --- editor and biographer

The roles of editor and biographer appear to place the writer in two neat categories, but in reality there are a number of subordinate roles which come into play once the work is published. In diverse ways the media reaches into my private writing world in the interests of introducing Anne Lister's world to a greater public, as the examples below illustrate.

Tutor

Dear Helena Whitbread,

I am an English student ... researching for my dissertation on how intimacy is conveyed in Eighteenth and early Nineteenth-Century letters. I am looking at how code, and other verbal techniques manage to create a closeness between correspondents, to make up for the physical distance between them. ... I would absolutely love to use some examples from Lister's coded letters too. It would be brilliant to hear any advice or thoughts you had on this.

Public speaker

From: Queen Mary, University of London
Subject: Autumn Symposium
Sent: 18.06.2012

We would be delighted if you would consider presenting a short (15-20 minute) paper in Panel 1 which would speak to the key themes identified above.

Radio talks

(*Woman's Hour*, November 2009)

Dear Helena

I phoned today and left a message on your answering machine. I wanted to confirm that we do want you to come to Manchester to take part in the discussion on Anne Lister this Friday, 6th November.

Television

Consultant for:

- the short film *A Marriage*, 1994, BBC Wales
- the film *The Secret Diaries of Miss Anne Lister*, 2010, made by Oxford Film and Television for BBC2

❦

Helena's view on lesbianism

Natasha

How did you feel about lesbianism before you started deciphering Anne's diaries?

Helena

This is a little hard to define. I understood, of course, about how one could have a 'crush' on another girl or woman. In my case, when I was about thirteen, I developed a crush on my science teacher at the all-girls Catholic Grammar School I attended. She was very good-looking and wore her hair in Veronica Lake fashion.

I also had a crush on a girl at the same school who was a couple of years older than me, but I never had sexual feelings for either of them. I just found them inextricably fascinating in some sort of obscure way.

When I was about sixteen a friend of mine came out as a lesbian and I remember that we (the group of friends with whom I attended the local youth club) were all a little shocked, not having had any previous idea of her sexual orientation.

In my later teens, I worked in a shop where one of my colleagues, Audrey, was a lesbian. She had quite a number of young women admirers /girl friends who often

called in at the shop to see her. She rode a motorbike and wore masculine clothes which, in the late forties, was something of an anomaly for a woman. On one occasion she made an amatory advance towards me, but I shied away nervously.

A second incident occurred when I was a student nurse at a children's hospital. A woman called Joyce developed strong romantic feelings for me and wanted us to work together, running a nursing home, when we were both qualified. I was intrigued by her and wondered whether or not I really did have sexual feelings for her, but it petered out before it began properly, as I left the hospital shortly afterwards.

A further experience occurred in the early 1950s which served to heighten my, slightly fearful, mystification about the lesbian world. Next door to my mother-in-law's house, in the small northern village in which we then lived, there was a woman in her mid-thirties who was the subject of much scurrilous gossip in the area. She had a lesbian lover who came for her in the evenings but did not call at the door. Instead, she stood waiting in the shadows across the road, a tall, mannish figure, dressed entirely in black masculine clothing, a sartorial style which served to enhance her 'otherness,' much in the same way that Anne Lister's adoption of all-black clothing did, over a hundred years earlier.

So, I think my feelings about lesbianism, prior to finding the Anne Lister journals were, as a very young woman, a mixture of wonderment at what appeared to me to be a strange, twilit world and nervousness at being invited to become a participant in that world.

As a mature woman, firmly established in a heterosexual marriage, I gave very little thought to my early tentative experiences of that other world, but was never condemnatory of those who inhabited it. I think my attitude was of the order of 'live and let live.'

<u>Natasha</u>

And how do you feel about lesbianism now, after your extensive work with Anne Lister's journals?

<u>Helena</u>

My education into what had largely been a closed world to me began in the 1980s. The early encounters which I had had with the lesbian world, all took place in the late 1940s and early 1950s.

For the next three decades I had no interaction with the lesbian world, a state of being which was radically altered in the early 1980s when my daughter 'came out' to me. And two years after that I discovered the Anne Lister journals. From that point on, I started to become involved in today's open society of lesbian women and the historical, closeted society of Anne Lister's world.

Almost three decades later my view on lesbianism has undergone a seismic change from those early feelings of what I have described as 'slightly fearful mystification.'

The lesbian world is now, to me, a place where I feel comfortable and, importantly, accepted. I gave them their history, in the figure of Anne Lister, the first modern lesbian, and in return they have given me their friendship and taught me that there is no 'black and white' approach to people's sexuality. It is not just a case of a person being either heterosexual or homosexual — there are, in fact, gradations of sexuality and that should be an acceptable fact of life.

Natasha
Did having a lesbian daughter fuel your interest in understanding Anne Lister?

Helena

I think perhaps it was the other way around. My daughter had 'come out' to me before I discovered the Anne Lister journals. My deep research into Anne's life over many years has helped me to understand my daughter's lesbianism, and has given me a great deal of insight into the difficulties of leading a lesbian life, albeit in different eras.

I found myself merging, in my mind, the characters of Anne Lister and my daughter in my reading of Anne's struggles to construct her lesbian identity in the face of a hostile world. I gained a great deal of empathy for my daughter's own struggles. I found I was living with two women in two very different eras whose point of connection, over two centuries, was their sexuality.

Natasha
Did any of Anne's revelations change your view of lesbianism?

Helena
Yes. As I say above, my views on lesbianism had drifted off into a sort of benign indifference, but the Anne Lister journals brought the subject into sharp focus for me.

At times I felt deeply moved by Anne's efforts to find a woman with whom she could share her life. Rather than dismissing her as a sexual predator in the way that some critics do, I found myself understanding her predicament and sympathising with her throughout the humiliations she suffered, both publicly and privately — not least those which her lover Mariana Lawton inflicted upon her. Having said that, I am not unaware of Anne's faults, of her snobbishness in particular, but here I will employ an old saying — 'To know all is to forgive all.'

౪ి౪
Books by Helena Whitbread

The Secret Diaries of Miss Anne Lister

Virago, London, 2010 — paperback and Kindle.

These remarkable diaries are a piece of lost lesbian history. Anne
Lister defied the role of womanhood seen in the novels of Jane
Austen: she was bold, fiercely independent, a landowner,
industrialist, traveller — and lesbian. She kept extensive diaries,
written partly in code, of her life and loves. The diaries have been
edited by Helena Whitbread, who spent years decoding and
transcribing them.

No Priest But Love

New York University Press, 1992.
Smith Settle, Otley, West Yorkshire, 1992.
Virago, London, 2015 — Kindle.

This journal is taken from the period 1824 to 1826, starting with
Anne's trip to Paris. It is through her amazingly frank and detailed
journals that we are able to enter into her adventurous life. The
chronicling of her passionate affairs with other women would have
startled her contemporaries. *'I love and only love the fairer sex,'* she
wrote. The explicit accounts of her sexual contacts have a power to
shock that has not diminished.

--- Media recognition ---

<u>Film</u>

A Skirt Through History (A Marriage) – BBC2 drama documentary, May 1994

The Secret Diaries of Miss Anne Lister – BBC2 film, May 2010

Revealing Anne Lister – BBC2 documentary, May 2010

<u>Radio</u>

Gentleman Jack from Halifax – BBC Radio 4 documentary, 2nd October 1993

The First Modern Lesbian – BBC Radio 4 Woman's Hour, 6th November 2009

<u>Theatre</u>

I Know My Own Heart – A Lesbian Regency Romance by Emma Donoghue, Cambridge 1991 – Dublin 1993

ℰℭℬ
Books by Natasha Holme

Lesbian Crushes at School:
A Diary on Growing Up Gay in the Eighties

In 1983 thirteen-year-old Natasha is in love with her French teacher, Miss Williams. When Natasha is cruelly banished from Miss Williams's class forever, the love develops into obsession ... stalking ... unhealthy behaviour ... and painfully misguided cries for attention.

This uncomfortable yet light-hearted memoir in diary form is primarily a record of obsession.

Natasha is a love-sick lesbian teenager in an all-girls school in the eighties, juggling her Latin homework, Bible study, a crush on Elaine Paige, and her suppressed sexuality. How can she make sense of it all?

But more importantly ... tormented by unrequited love ... how can Natasha make Miss Williams love her back? Take a sneaky peek inside. ...

Lesbian Crushes and Bulimia:
A Diary on How I Acquired my Eating Disorder

In 1989 nineteen-year-old Natasha is obsessively in love with her former teacher, Miss Williams. The tattoo she flashes around says so. Natasha meets Alex, a girl her own age, who questions her about the tattoo. An awkward romance is born.

In this real-life teenage diary Natasha records her panic at a looming LESBIAN relationship. To lose some excess fat, she starves herself of food ... whilst working in a chip shop. And just to make sure she's gay, Natasha drags five boys into bed in the space of a week, a sin for which the sexuality police threaten to kick her out of the university Lesbian and Gay Society.

In this coming out story and love story, Natasha struggles with clumsy attempts at heterosexuality, the sickening effects of weight loss techniques, disapproving shaven-headed lesbians, and sexual harassment in the chip shop.

Lesbian Crushes in France: A Diary on Screwing Up my Year Abroad

In 1990 twenty-year-old Natasha finds herself in France on her university year abroad. She is ANGRY. Everyone should be a lesbian, or she will punish them for their oversight (particularly her bemused fellow English assistant friend, Ange).

The *frites* and the *pâtisseries* are not helping Natasha recover from her bulimia. And the door-to-door Mormon missionaries are bedevilling her reluctant search for God.

Natasha does not respond well to the frosty demands of the headmaster of the school where she is teaching.

She passes her time befriending a pair of thieving drop-outs on the run from the law, skinning up grilled banana skins, dodging flashers, and hitch-hiking around Europe.